The Word for the Day

65 Years of Bob Steele's Wit and Wisdom on Mispronunciation

by Bob Steele and Phil Steele

Illustrations by Bob Steele

To David D'Eramo —
My very best !
Bob Steele H.S.G.

Connecticut River Press
Newington, Connecticut
2002

ISBN 0-9706573-1-5

Designed by Cheryl Dauphin

DEDICATION

Hartford's new Learning Corridor, a 16-acre campus of magnet schools adjacent to Trinity College, includes two regional high school programs — the Greater Hartford Academy of the Arts and the Greater Hartford Academy of Math and Science.

In commemoration of the 150th anniversary of the publication of *Uncle Tom's Cabin*, Hartford's Harriet Beecher Stowe Center sponsored a program March 9, 2002 at the Learning Corridor's Black Box Theater. The highlight of the program was a spectacular student performance. Music Director Michael Wilson presented an hour-long segment of his *Writing Pictures: The Harriet Beecher Stowe Experience*. Although the music was good enough to be on Broadway, its magic went far beyond the music. The story is about the American experience, our long, often painful struggle for freedom and equality of all people. But it was the performers who made it live and underscored its meaning.

If the peoples of the world, with all our races, cultures, languages and pronunciations, are ever to live in peace and share the pursuit of happiness, these students, in their diversity, their unity and their spirit, show us the way. We dedicate this book to all the teachers and schools of America, and especially, to the students of the Greater Hartford Academy of the Arts.

ACKNOWLEDGMENTS

The authors gratefully acknowledge the permission of Spoonwood Press to utilize some of the material from *Bob Steele: A Man and His Humor* (1980) and *Bob Steele's 50th Anniversary: An Affectionate Memoir*, by Jane Moskowitz and Jane Gillard (1986). Our thanks to the Honorable Joseph Steinberg, now a Senior Judge of the Connecticut Superior Court, who brought both of the earlier books to print through Spoonwood and who strongly encouraged this new book.

It would be very hard to overstate our debt to Rob Kyff. When I started reading Rob's syndicated column on words in the Hartford Courant, I thought his name was pronounced *Kiff*. When I found out that it rhymes with *knife*, I used it as the Word for the Day. Rob was extremely generous with his time in reviewing our manuscript. His students at West Hartford's Kingswood-Oxford School are lucky to have so insightful a teacher. His keen insight and contributions with all aspects of the book have been invaluable, and his own very readable and humorous book on words, *Word Up!* (Writers Club Press, 2000) has been an inspiration.

Some years ago I began reviewing the words on my Saturday show that I had used during the week, but whatever I jotted them down on often seemed to get lost. For more than ten years beginning in the early 1980s "Newington Bob" Williams of Newington kept track of The Word for the Day each day and called me Saturday mornings to help me out on those frequent occasions when I couldn't find my list.

Our thanks to the staff of the Hartford Public Library and to city tourist officials in places like Ypsilanti, Michigan; Mobile, Alabama; Biloxi, Mississippi; Belgrade, Maine; Helsinki, Finland and Brisbane and Canberra, Australia for helping to confirm and clarify local pronunciations.

Steele family members Robert H. Steele and Paul Steele reviewed the manuscript and contributed indispensable advice and support.

Cheryl Dauphin's creative work in designing the dust jacket and the page layout was always insightful and responsive to the needs of the book and has helped greatly to enhance its content. Jack Meier, Dave Caron and Carol Gilbert of Connecticut River Press have been a pleasure to work with. Jack's enthusiastic support for the project from our first contact was a strong boost to its fruition. The enthusiasm and expertise of Bob Dunn and Tim Gaillard of 21st Century Media have also helped to bring the project to market and to ensure its success.

INTRODUCTION
By James F. English, Jr.

I grew up in West Hartford in the years just before World War II and like most kids was addicted to the radio: Jack Armstrong, the Lone Ranger and Fred Allen. I even built a rickety crystal set with earphones so I could listen after hours; I hitched it to my bed springs for an antenna.

So I was very familiar with the sound of Bob Steele's resonant voice on "Strictly Sports," and it was a big event for me when he took over "The Morning Watch," G. Fox's enormously popular morning program on WTIC, the Travelers Insurance Companies station. It represented the essence of Hartford, and for the people of Connecticut, it was like all of today's morning TV shows combined.

This morning show reached hundreds of thousands of faithful listeners between 1943 and 1991, giving Bob, for nearly half a century, one of the largest audience shares ever enjoyed by any radio personality in a major U.S. broadcast market. His 65 years of continuous broadcasting on the same station have made him the longest running radio personality in the business, and he still does his show the first Saturday of the month nine months a year. In 1995 his success earned him a place as one of the early inductees into the national Radio Hall of Fame in Chicago.

Radio broadcasting was less than sixteen years old when Bob joined WTIC in 1936, and his enormously popular sports and morning shows helped shape both genres for the remainder of the century. He had developed his verbal skills over a decade of humorous sportswriting—the Maestro of Phun and Philosophy, one magazine called him. His morning show, which originally aired from 7 to 8 a.m. and gradually expanded to four and a half hours, brought out the full breadth of his talent.

Bob opened the show with the crowing rooster, chirping birds, pealing bells, barking hounds and galloping horses of Voelker's "A Hunt in the Black Forest." Its rousing music literally helped wake up the entire region, from the Berkshires to Long Island Sound, and he closed the program with "The Second Connecticut Regiment March" "to help you step lively through your day," he explained. Indeed, as former Governor Ella Grasso once observed, Bob's entire show was devoted to "brightening our mornings as we sought the strength to face a new day," and in the process he became "as much a part of our lives as the morning sunrise."

Bob filled the show with news, weather, sports and music, including popular tunes of the day and his own selections, which ran from classic oldies to bands and instrumentals. But it was his running commentary and special features that kept listeners glued to the radio so they wouldn't miss his latest joke, funny story, humorous aside or outrageous pun. He had a comedian's gift for timing, could make people laugh out loud at even the corniest jokes, and had a completely natural and self-effacing manner which made people comfortable. Listeners invariably commented that they felt as though he were talking directly to them, had actually come into their home and sat down at the breakfast table or followed them through the house as they got ready for work.

Bob talked affectionately about his wife and four sons and impishly about the gallery of fictitious relatives whom he invented to illustrate what seemed like virtually every foible of the human race. He shared his own favorite and, in some cases original, recipes, provided constant time checks, threw in an occasional limerick to make a point, read letters—both zany and serious—from listeners, reminded people to take their keys and wallets as they went out the door, helped them through traffic jams, and explained how to pronounce a frequently mispronounced word correctly. He reveled in picking the underdog in sporting events and then joking about his poor record as a prognosticator. He kidded about his boxing career, in which he had 52 amateur and 18 pro fights, losing all but four of the professional bouts with two draws. (He claims he was robbed on 14 occasions.) And he talked wistfully of having had to drop out of high school three times to help support his family. Nevertheless, he said he was the only kid in his neighborhood to go to college before graduating from high school (he used to get his hair cut for a dime at the local barber college), a feat he accomplished in 1929, just in time to take part in the Depression (he also predicted there would be no Depression).

The morning show quickly became the "franchise" for WTIC, developing a long waiting list for advertisers. One moving and storage sponsor, who waited for over two years to get on the program, described the show's commercial attraction very simply in 1958. He said that when he pulled up to a stop light on his way to work during the summer, when most of the cars had their windows open, almost everyone in the other cars was listening to Bob Steele.

Bob, in fact, never did make it to college, yet he has received honorary degrees from universities to go with his highly-prized H.S.G. (High School Graduate), and it would be difficult to meet a more intelligent or polished gentleman. In addition to a rich, resonant speaking voice, he has an exceptional ear for language and he made himself a student of words and grammar. He can imitate accents and dialects with great accuracy, and he amazes native foreign language speakers with his ability to pick up the accents, inflections and intonations of their languages and rattle off names and phrases in perfect Russian, Polish, French, Italian and German. One of his most delightful offerings was the periodic reading of the hilariously understated British farce "The Lion and Albert," which he did in an authentic Lancastrian brogue.

Bob's love for the spoken word led him to create "The Word for the Day," a daily feature in which he examined a frequently mispronounced, misunderstood or incorrectly used word, and patiently explained its correct pronunciation, often clarifying its meaning or usage with the help of an amusing story, observation or one-liner. Bob has run the feature for over 60 years, establishing an unequalled reputation and record as a radio lexicologist. Unfortunately, no complete record of "The Word for the Day" exists, but Bob and his son Phil have painstakingly combed through the notes and recordings, as well as memories, which do remain to create the present book. In it they have succeeded in reproducing both the substance and the light touch that helped hundreds of thousands of New Englanders improve their speaking ability and deepen their appreciation of our language without ever breaking a sweat.

So far as I know, features like "The Word for the Day" never quite made it on TV; they just weren't visual enough. But I'm glad to see that they are flourishing in the newspaper and on the internet; my morning invariably begins with a cup of coffee and, then, a cheery e-mail message from "A Word A Day." It's a pleasant and reassuring way to start the morning. And, for me, and so many others, it all began with Bob Steele.

Mr. English is President Emeritus of Trinity College in Hartford, Connecticut and a former Chairman of The Connecticut Bank & Trust Company.

FOREWORD
By Rob Kyff

I first came to New England 25 years ago as a rookie high-school English teacher. Fresh from Minnesota, I was totally unfamiliar with the institutions and personalities of Connecticut. While surfing the radio dial one autumn morning, I discovered Bob Steele and his Word for the Day. "Hey, listen to this," I called to my wife. "Some guy is giving advice about pronunciation!"

Some guy, indeed.

To me, a fledgling English teacher who was desperately trying to shepherd squirmy ninth graders through the treacherous thickets of grammar, usage and pronunciation, Bob's lessons were a warm hand on my shoulder. His daily lessons reassured me that other people cared about speaking proper English and that my earnest efforts with students might not be entirely in vain.

Hartford suddenly seemed a more civilized, more literate and more human place, and I knew I had found a kindred spirit.

That kindred spirit has taught me much during the past quarter century. I've learned that I (an English teacher, no less!) have been mispronouncing many words all my life - that *flaccid* is FLAK-sid not FLAS-id; *err* is ur not air; *bade* is bad not bade; *coup de grâce* is koo d' GRAHS not koo d' GRAH, and *dais* is DAY-is not DY-is.

More important, I've learned from Bob to sweeten the grapefruit of proper English with the sugar of laughter. Bob's warm wit and lighthearted approach to language have taught me how to leaven my own classroom presentations (though my students have always insisted my puns are much worse than Bob's).

When I began writing the "Word Watch" column for *The Hartford Courant* ten years ago, Bob became my model of the Populist Grammarian. Translating complex linguistic concepts and rules into clear and engaging language is difficult, and no one does this better than Bob. Overexplain and you bore your readers; oversimplify and you mislead them. Bob strikes just the right balance of diction and delight. This book exemplifies that balance. It is, first and foremost, an authoritative guide to precise pronunciation and more, considering not only the proscriptions of scholars but the preferences of average people. But it's also a joyful escapade, sparkling with delicious anecdotes, fascinating asides and snappy wisecracks. As Bob tells us how to pronounce, his own words pounce.

Most of us are familiar with Henry Higgins, the professor in the musical My Fair Lady, and his laborious, tedious efforts to teach correct pronunciation to Eliza Doolittle: "ay" not "eye," "e" not "ow," "the rain in Spain," etc.

Bob is neither laborious nor tedious. He's melodious and felicitous. He gives pronunciation, as Eliza Doolittle might have put it, "a good nime."

He's Henry Higgins with a heart.

Rob Kyff, whose syndicated column about words appears in *The Hartford Courant*, teaches at the Kingswood-Oxford School in West Hartford and is the author of *Word-Up* (2000).

THE FIRST WORD FOR THE DAY
By Bob Steele, H.S.G.

> *It is easier to overlook any question of speech than to
> trouble about it, but then it is also easier to snort or
> neigh, growl or to "meaow," than to articulate and
> intonate ... the innumerable differentiated, discriminated
> units of sound and sense that lend themselves to audible
> production, to enunciation, to intonation: those innu-
> merable units that have, each, an identity, a quality, an
> outline, a shape, a clearness, a fineness, a sweetness, a
> richness, that have in a word, a value, which it is open
> to us, as lovers of our admirable English tradition, or
> as cynical traitors to it, to preserve or destroy.*
>
> HENRY JAMES

Henry James wouldn't have thought much of one member of
our family—Uncle Stainless—who has absolutely no concern for the
way he pronounces anything, and has probably never heard of Henry.
The way Uncle Stainless sees it, if he wants to say mis-CHEE-vee-us or
ES-kyoo-layt or JOO-luh-ree or MEM-uh-ruh-**BEEL**-yuh, why should
anyone else care? There's something very appealing about this attitude.
Sometimes ignorance can be bliss. Needless to say, though, Uncle
Stainless will not be getting a copy of this book.

The first Word for the Day has to be *hog*, September 30, 1936.
Let me tell you the story.

It all began with my love of motorcycles. I started riding one in
Kansas City when I was 13 and used it to earn some money delivering for
a pharmacy and for Western Union. Most exciting to me was motorcycle
racing and hill climbing competition. At 14 I was sending motorcycle
news to a national magazine, *MotorCycling*. One day in 1931 I got hurt
in a time trial on a half-mile track in Stockton, California. By
coincidence the stadium announcer became ill. I knew all about the
motorcycle races, so they let me announce them on the public address
system. That was the start of my announcing over a microphone.

At age 12 I'd built my first crystal radio set, and I listened to the
announcers so much that I sort of patterned my speech after them. I was
conscious of speaking clearly and talking to a large number of people.
I used to practice in my room, reading advertising copy from *the
Saturday Evening Post* ... never dreaming I'd ever really get a job in radio.

While working in a California bean field for the WPA in May of 1936, I got a telegram from a friend who was promoting motorcycle racing in Hartford, asking me to do the announcing for the summer season. Jobs were hard to come by, so I took off for Hartford. At the end of the racing season, I was getting a ride back to California with one of the motorcycle racers. It was the last day of September and I had nothing to do until my ride left. I was 25 years old.

Radio then was just entering its heyday and I was fascinated by it. Radio was live and it was exciting. It offered a huge and growing range of programs that informed, entertained, educated, and stimulated the imagination—from news and music to quiz shows and talent shows, from comedies to mysteries, from national news to play-by-play sporting events; from soap operas and Hollywood gossip to FDR's fireside chats; and from adventure serials to serious drama. All of this, mind you, was performed live.

The networks built elaborate new facilities in New York, Chicago and Hollywood, and even many local stations had studios big enough to hold entire orchestras. And, after initially depending heavily on recruiting nationally known entertainers from the stage and screen, radio had begun to create its own entertainment stars. It was beginning to produce serious broadcast journalists, and was forging unique bonds between listeners and their favorite programs and personalities.

Radio, in short, had become an integral part of American life, an alluring reflection and expression of our dynamic country and everything that was modern about the world. The radio console became one of the most prized possessions in the homes of the 1930s. Early risers turned it on first thing in the morning, homemakers listened to it during the day, children monopolized it after school, and whole families gathered around it to listen to their favorite shows each night.

Adding to the excitement was the speed with which radio had taken hold. It had been less than sixteen years since KDKA in Pittsburgh broadcast the 1920 presidential election returns and signaled the birth of the broadcasting industry. In that incredibly short time, radio had dramatically changed the way Americans communicated. In the process, radio had become America's main form of entertainment. It had become a chief source of news and information, it had become the country's most powerful advertising medium, and it had become a new force for influencing the way Americans thought, spoke and acted.

How could I resist? I had always wanted to be a radio announcer, but public address announcing for motorcycle races was about as far as I got. I had done a little bit of motorcycle and auto racing description on a station in Los Angeles called KGFJ, but I wasn't a staff man. I knew nothing about radio work. I just knew enough to talk about the races.

Wanting to get into radio, I did go to WDRC during that summer in '36 for an audition. They gave me some news to read. "We'll call you." The old story. So I gave it up. I thought I'd never make it because I'd taken auditions before at several LA stations—small stations—and I never made it. By that last day in September I'd pretty much given up the idea. But I had this time to kill, and I was in downtown Hartford.

About 3 o'clock in the afternoon, I went to the Princess Theatre on State Street. The theater is no longer there, of course, gone like all the other downtown movie houses. The girl in the cage said, "There's a mystery on. Go in now and you'll ruin it. If you wait about twenty-five minutes, you can get in at the beginning of it."

So I walked across the Old State House lawn to the Travelers building on Central Row. So help me, I walked right in and asked the elevator operator for WTIC. He took me up to the sixth floor in the Grove Street building. I went in and just asked, "Do you need any announcers here?"

This was in 1936. You couldn't buy a job in those days. People were starving to death. It was the height of the Depression. And WTIC was not just another radio station. Owned by the Travelers Insurance Companies, it was a 50,000-watt giant, the top station in Connecticut, and one of the premier stations in the country.

Despite all of this, Fred Wade, the chief announcer, said, "As a matter of fact, we're looking for an announcer. We just auditioned thirteen guys about an hour ago." He looked me over and said, "We'll give you a shot at it if you want to go in." I went in and gave it a shot. They gave me some news to read and some musical programs to announce. They wanted to see if I knew anything about composers like Bach, Beethoven and all those fellows. I'd never heard of them, but they gave me the sheet and I read them just the way they looked. I didn't know how to pronounce them. I had never gone to college.

But I had learned something about words and about playing with words, even if I didn't always know how to pronounce them. For several years I'd been writing a humorous column for a national magazine, *The Motorcyclist*, that I called "Poppings of the Day" by Prof. Popper. Later I began using my real name and the column became "Stalling Around With Steele."

When I talked to the boss, Paul Morency, after the audition, he seemed to like my sense of humor. "If we can get the Midwestern accent out of your speech," he decided, "we'll give you a trial." I found out he was from Illinois himself and he knew a Western or Midwestern accent when he heard one. "Back here we say hahg, for example. H-o-g is hahg. It isn't hawg."

In the days ahead, I became very interested in correct pronunciation and usage, and I never lost my interest. I may owe my career to it. Mr. Morency was apparently reasonably satisfied with my progress and I stayed around for the next 65 years. After I was put on "The G. Fox Hour"—7:00 to 8:00 in the morning, six days a week, in March of '43, I tried sharing my verbal self-improvement with my listeners and The Word for the Day became a regular feature and continued well after "Poppings of the Day" was history.

Trying to get it right didn't just help me keep my job. I also saw it as a great responsibility. Before radio, news and entertainment came primarily from the written word and the theater. Pronunciation simply wasn't that much of an issue. But radio focused new attention on the spoken word. Once you had professionals broadcasting to millions of people, pronunciation and usage inevitably stood out and became more important.

Dictionaries "record" pronunciation. We've recorded mispronunciation, and thus judged it as well—an undertaking that may seem arrogant and presumptuous to some. Who's to say what correct pronunciation is? Before 1961 the only pronunciation you could find in any dictionary for *alleged* was uh-LEJD—two syllables. Then Webster "recorded" uh-LEJ-id as well. Why shouldn't it? Probably a majority of Americans now pronounce it with three syllables. While the gradual change toward simplicity and ease of speech that, for example, makes so many leave the *r* out of *February* will continue, ignorance and carelessness are another matter.

Taking care in the way we use and pronounce words enhances our ability to communicate with each other. It may never have occurred to you that every time you say anything, you're confirming or varying a cultural pattern, and adding to the accumulation we call pronunciation. While American English is constantly changing, educated people should know what the standards are. The risk of not knowing is not only that your ability to communicate will suffer, but that you will make a less favorable impression on others than you would like. However fair or unfair it may seem, people still judge you to a large degree by how you speak.

My experience tells me that most people pay little or no attention to their pronunciation—at least until you challenge it! But most will usually welcome guidance from those who pay more attention to such matters. So that's what we have here. We've been paying attention, and we don't think all pronunciations are created equal. Some of what we offer here is little more than our own opinion, but we hope it will at least get you to pay more attention yourself.

When Phil first spoke to a publisher many years ago about publishing this book, he was cautioned that anyone who owns a dictionary has no need for a book on pronunciation. Most everyone has a dictionary, yes, and it's a wonderful reference tool, but the number of people who read or browse it surely could fit into a phone booth with enough room left over for a camel. How many people even consult it from time to time in order to check a pronunciation? Dictionaries are heavy, dull and dry. They have small print. You usually have to consult the pronunciation key at the bottom of the page to figure out the symbols, and trying to make sense of all those squiggly lines is a job in itself. And you would probably never pick up a dictionary in order to hunt randomly for words you might be mispronouncing. Although we make no claim to being complete or exhaustive, we hope this is a book that puts a great many common mispronunciations and a few usage errors in one place and that you will feel invited to read it.

If you enjoy this book, please look for our sequel, *How to File Your Nails Alphabetically*, in which we'll tell you how to pronounce Pszczyna (Poland) and Llwchr (Wales).

FROM POPPINGS OF THE DAY TO THE WORD FOR THE DAY
By Phil Steele

As well as I thought I knew my father, there was a lot I didn't discover until I began helping him with this book. The story he shares with us is only part of it. The Word for the Day started long before he walked into WTIC on September 30, 1936. As I searched his voluminous scrapbooks and records from the 1920s and '30s, I began to see how Bob Steele's love of words and wit grew into the personality New Englanders came to love.

Dad had to grow up fast in the '20s. His parents divorced when he was five, and as an only child he and his mother had to struggle to make ends meet. Dropping out of school several times in order to work, he needed six years to earn his diploma from Westport High School in Kansas City. He had his first motorcycle when he was 13, and used it to deliver telegrams and prescriptions.

Motorcycle riders were never called bikers back then, just riders or motorcycle men, corner benders or the sickling fraternity, The ladies sometimes called themselves cyclettes. Those who competed were called broadsiders, hill climbers, endurance riders, sidecar racers, road racers, short track racers, long track racers (a.k.a. short trackers and long trackers) and stunt riders. A motorcycle was called a machine or a sickle, and sometimes a crate or a crock but rarely just a cycle; hog for Harleys came later.

Of course, Dad used his sickle the way any 13-year-old would and soon got to know most of the other riders in the Kansas City area. The motorcycling crowd of the 1920s didn't fit the tattooed, bearded and long-haired stereotype of today, and most couldn't have afforded leather jackets even if they'd been available back then, but the riders of the '20s were, if not unkempt, at least an untamed, thrill-seeking bunch. Yes, Dad was a joyrider. He raced, he entered hill-climbing events, did reckless stunts and was as fun-loving and foolhardy as any young man with a fast, powerful and exciting machine would inevitably be. By the time he was 21, he'd survived injuries from motorcycle crack-ups that landed him in the hospital 14 times!

As fortune had it though, all that life and energy took a creative turn as well. One of the nation's popular sports magazines of the day, *MotorCycling*, featured news from the many cycling clubs all over the country. But it had no news from Kansas City and Dad saw an opportunity. He wrote a piece on the motorcycle men he knew and sent it to the bi-weekly in Chicago. They didn't know he was only 14, and wrote back offering him $7.50 an issue to contribute a regular column, a fair piece of change in those days, especially for a teen helping to support his mother.

But Dad's news from KC wasn't quite the same as what other contributors were sending in. A funny thing happened on the way to the motorcycle forum—literally. He found he couldn't write for very long without giving his words a humorous, even manic, "lilt and tilt," as one of his editors put it. That was his style. Out came puns and animated word-play. He called the column "Krazy Kracks from K.C." Long before his invention of Uncle Stainless and a whole extended family from Aunt Bessamer to Grandpa Rusty, his very name fostered inventiveness with language. In 1929 Sun-Maid promoted its 5-cent boxes of raisins with the slogan "Had your iron today?" When he and his mother opened a sandwich shop, their sign read, "Had your iron today? If not, have a Steele sandwich!"

After the Depression hit, Dad went to southern California to find work and again got to know everyone in the world of motor-cycling. The offices of another national magazine, *The Motorcyclist*, were in L.A. and he began contributing a column entitled "Poppings of the Day by Prof. Popper." "Poppings of the Day" was a play on one of the era's movie house newsreels, "Topics of the Day." Like some of the noises that come out of sickles, Poppings came out of Dad's motor-cycling experience and perspective on life. In the '40s he began using his real name instead of Prof. Popper and the column became "Stalling Around with STEELE."

Dad reported on motorcycle racing and hill-climbing events and the riders and their machines. Often it was straight and serious stuff. But a great deal of it was humor. Words became his skill, his capital. The Maestro of Phun and Philosophy, one magazine called him. In a real sense, Dad's Word for the Day came out of his Poppings of the Day.

———

The following reproductions from "Poppings of the Day by Prof. Popper" and "Stalling Around with STEELE" in The Motorcyclist *offered humorous relief during the Depression and WWII not only on pronunciation but on such subjects as the 1938 hurricane, rationing and the draft.*

POPPINGS of the DAY
by PROF. POPPER

February, 1936

And now to get around to the first important thing I can think of; I wonder why, when we motorcyclists break into print, they always spell our names wrong? Was reading a clipping from a Savannah newspaper recently telling about the 200 mile road race there and was maddened slightly by the headline: "KRATZ WINS RACE." His name is KRETZ, not KRATZ, as I have known him for some time and he's a small town boy from Corona, California and is a whiz of a rider. Then in the article itself they called him EARL KRATZ. His name is ED, not EARL. Reminds me of Miny Waln, the west coast racer and long track national champ in 1930. His name was misspelled every time a printer got next to it. It varied from "Minny Wilp" to "Ming Wong." (Very bad case of wong spelling, wot?) The latter spelling appeared in an Oakland paper once and since then Miny has frequently been referred to as the "Chinese Champion." He's Welsh-German, by the way, and pronounces the Miny part of his name with a long "i," as in "mine."

July, 1936

I was going through Hartford, Conn., once upon a time and I met Fred Marsh, Indian dealer there and quite a long track racer since 1924. Fred got on the subject of grammar and we got to talking about what a different meaning a sentence could take on if a different word were emphasized each time it was repeated. "Take the sentence: 'What am I doing?'" Fred said. And I began: "**WHAT** am I doing? What **AM** I doing? What am **I** doing? What am I **DOING**?" Whereupon Wise Cracker Marsh broke in: "If you ask me, professor, you're making a damn fool of yourself!"

August, 1937

HELLO, BOYS, GIRLS and people of the vast motor and cycle audience. Pardon me for being late with my stuff for last issue. I was out playing golf, got caught in a sand trap and was there 19 days taking 3,777 ¼ strokes. The quarter stroke was for the swing I cut short when some bird told me he saw me smack the pill onto the green with the first stroke almost three weeks before. Instead of the ball, I had been batting at a stump of white birch all that time and broke 618 clubs, 32 rake handles, 4 electric razors, the front forks of my 1922 big valve Ex. and a short beer. I think it was that way but I may have to check up to be sure. Ordinarily, I play a swell game. I'll never forget the day I was playing Joe Petrali. I was going great. Had a neat 93 for the first eight holes and then something happened and I went all to pieces on the ninth.

May, 1938

One of our motorcycle boys took up art. He sent the professor this sample of his work and it seems good enough for reproduction. It is entitled, "Three white swans eating marshmallows in a snow storm."

September, 1938

Another note from "Walt" of Portland, Oregon, wants the Prof.'s advice on a matter concerning the ancient and somewhat nefarious pastime of "stud poker." Well, for nine successive years I won the Nobel award for distinguished poker playing, and every year since 1923 I have had the pleasure of receiving the Pulitzer prize for concealing cards up my sleeve, so I guess that qual-

ifies me to answer Walt's query. This avid "Poppings" fan wants to know if there's any truth in the statement that: "A first rate poker player will always be successful in business." No, my friend, there isn't much sense in that adage. A first rate poker player doesn't need a business!

October, 1938

What with all the war talk in Europe, trees falling all about me here in New England as a result of the hurricane, and my typewriter standing in twelve feet of water, I'm not sure I can sufficiently compose myself to dash off this month's Poppings but I'll try. Not having anything to ride the editor about this time I don't know just how to start. He seems to have got himself out of that Corrigan mix-up which appeared a couple of issues back, and he has just sent me a check for $1.34 and some cigar coupons for my last article, so I really don't think a bawling out would be justified. Those cigar coupons are pretty valuable to me as I need only 655 more to get a book on how to put out brush fires with an orange stick. This may sound silly to some of you but when you consider I travel a lot and always carry an orange stick to clean my nails with, I could do a great service if I happened onto a fire or something.

June, 1939 (Ladies edition)
By Mrs. Prof. Popper

Wouldn't you just know it would happen this way on the day that I have to write a column for his nibs? The baby has chewed up every pencil in the house, the police dog is using the typewriter to rattle off his weekly report to the chief of police and the Professor has used up all the stationery making those *!#*%! folding airplanes and sailing them out the window. But the column must go through (I really don't see any sense in it, but that's what the Prof. says) so I'm scratching this out on the bottom of the wash tub with a safety pin, and will roll it out to Mr. Billings like a hoop. I guess you can see by now that I'm crazy, too, girls, but after all why shouldn't I be? It's fun, and besides you have to be to live with the Prof. I always say.

I was tickled, really girls, when I read in the old man's chatter of last month that I was to have the privilege of "knocking out" a column for this issue, as he so aptly put it. I say "aptly" because "knocking out" Poppings of the Day is an appropriate expression. You should see him sit down at the typewriter to write the stuff. He gets over in a corner, has me introduce him to the baby and "Flat Foot" (the police dog), gets up and bows all over the room while clasping his hands above his head, then goes back to his corner and leads rights and lefts to all parts of the typewriter like he was tearing into Joe Louis—or rather like Joe Louis was tearing into him. This exhibition is short lived, however, as every time he gets to the end of a line the bell rings (like a typewriter bell will do at the end of a line) and the Prof. makes for the divan to lie down for a minute, usually going to sleep. Then, when I shake the mop in his map to get him up he awakes with a start and yells, "Where's dat bum? Lemme at 'im! I'll kill 'im! What happened? I ain't been robbed again, have I?" And that, girls, is how he "knocks out" a column. Well, anyway, as I said, I was tickled to learn that I was to write this one for this June number of ours. I figured it would be a lot less work than acting as the Prof.'s second.

Stalling Around with Steele

January, 1943

WHEN ARTHUR WELCH wired me a post card collect at my two-room mansion in Wethersfield, Conn. and told me I had been selected by the Board of Rumors to be an Associate Editor of The Motorcyclist, a celebration was prompted. I gathered my wife and two small boys in my arms and set out to have a big time, but in view of the ban on pleasure driving here in the East, we had to leave the sidehack outfit in the garage. It's a combination of two piano boxes, but we like to call it a garage.) Inasmuch as we live only a block away from a big state highway, I took the little family and seven cucumber sandwiches down to the side of the road and had a sort of picnic. We sat there all afternoon and just watched the car go by. (That's no misprint.) Nobody around here drives, or sickles, any more. Unless it's virtually an emergency.

April, 1943

I feel so bad I may soon be joining the man in Room 126. You heard what happened to him. A guy in 127 called the desk and said, "I just heard a shot in Room 126 followed by the sound of a body slumping to the floor!" So, the clerk sent the house dick up to 126 right away. He knocked, but got no answer, so he forced the door. Inside, he smelled gun smoke. Finding nothing in the room, he entered the bath room and there, lying on the tile floor, a bullet hole in his head and a .45 in his hand, was a dead man. The man in 126. The detectiff knelt down and listened to the man's heart, for a sign of life. No life. He put a mirror in front of the man's lips. But no breath clouded the glass. He lifted the man's arm, felt his pulse. No pulse. He let go and the arm flopped, lifeless, to the floor. "Definitely 4F!," said hawk-shaw, as he turned away.

May, 1943

Am I steamed up? Did you see that biography of your good friend and mine (ME) in last month's magazine? The editor dashes if off and every time he states that I did this or that he has to add the phrase: "HE says." He has to bring out the truth that I sent all that information in myself. Sure, all biographies are based on what the subject tells the author. Most of them, anyway. But the author doesn't come right out and say so. He makes out like he discovered all the dope himself without even speaking with the guy whose biog. he's penning. It's one of the little unwritten laws and courtesies of the writing profession. I should know. I'm a writer. I wrote Anthony Adverse. But I put the wrong address on the envelope and the letter went to the dead letter office.

Also, the editor (Welch, I believe his name is) said I had a son named Bob, Jr. Well, I'll have the ed know that I never DID have a son named Junior. That's one name I can't go for. I suppose I'll make all the Juniors mad now by saying this, but I'll name my boys **straight**. If they turn out to be crooked, that's THEIR business. Just for the record, my young gremlins are named Robert Hampton and Paul Alan. Well, that's enough name calling for now.

*   *   *

Speaking of hamburger, and things to eat, we had a chicken for dinner last week but we almost didn't get to eat it. My wife had never killed a chicken but wouldn't admit it to me. She was out in the back yard for an hour, trying to get up nerve enough to wring its neck. She couldn't do it. She got hold of a hatchet but couldn't get the chick to hold still on the block. Finally, she came in the house and confessed she had duped me when we were married.

She didn't know how to decapitate a Plymouth Rock. She cried and I told her it was all right, that we'll get along somehow. After I forgave her, I went out in the yard, cornered the chicken, told it four jokes and it LAUGHED its head off!

June, 1943

Letter from a Mr. J. A. Foster, Minneapolis, wants to know if I remember the first time I was on the air, and the answer is "Yes, definitely." It was in 1917 in Kansas City. I was six years old and was in the Shubert Theatre with my mother. We were poor as church mice and twice as fond of cheese, but it was a matinee and besides I got in as a halfwit at half price. A hypnotist was doing his stuff on the stage when we walked in and Mom and I had just sat down when the Svengali asked if there was a small boy in the audience who would assist him in his next exhibition of the supernatural. Mom said I should go ahead as someone might throw a thin one on the stage after the act and maybe I could beat the hypnotist to it. I fairly leaped to the stage and was immediately requested to lie down on a table, which I did willingly as I had been up all night the night before playing poker with my six-year-old cronies. I figured here was a chance to grab a small nap. Then, this smart guy in the tuxedo with the white tie, white gloves, white spats and the white Christmas proceeded to hypnotize me. Alakazam! Like that he had me hypnotized and stiff as a shirt just back from the laundry (a shirt you had requested be finished with NO STARCH). Then, Mom told me later, an assistant in a monkey suit removed the table from under me and there I was, horizontal, about four feet off the floor. And ... that's all there is to the story. That's the first time I was on the air.

June, 1947

Letters this month from Arthur Harrison Outloud and his brother Fork Ryan Outloud protest the inconsiderate actions of some few motorcyclists. The Brothers Outloud, pedestrians by nature, are loud in their criticism of riders who sneak up on unsuspecting foot travelers and race their motors, scaring the victims out of seven years of development.

* * *

The matter has been referred to the United States Inferior Court and, if not acted upon favorably by that august body, will be taken to the lowest court in the land or some september body. Whatever the disposition of this case, trust me to give you a typically biased and prejudiced Steele report in a subsequent issue.

October, 1947

Letter from a young street sweeper's apprentice in Las Vegas, New Jersey, wants me to ask if anyone has an apartment for him and his motorcycle. Although apartments are as rare as a hen's bridgework these days, this chap feels that someone in this vast reader's audience must have a little place he'd rent out. He's willing to leave the motorcycle outside if the landlord insists, but at least wants a place big enough to sleep in and turn over a couple of times each night. He used to be a pitcher for the Yanks and often tosses all night. If any of you folks can help this young man, contact me, Bahb Ctiehll, Stalling-on-the-Hudson, Connecticut.

November, 1947

Heavens! My youngest son, Phil, aged 3, has just parked his motorcycle and come running into my arms with the dreadful news that they have just fired Big Bigsby the Butcher, who works at our favorite shop down the corner. They finally discovered that he was taking a shortcut home every night.

March, 1948

Several complaints in my mail this month. Readers are hollering their heads off. Here's one from Huey Hill of Louisville (he's a Talon scout for a zipper factory down there) who says: "Your jokes REEK, Steele. I'm getting up a petition to have you run out of the country. I warn you, Steele, I'm going to leave no stone unthrown in an effort to have you blacklisted from the dignified and respectable profession of journalism."

* * *

Now there's what I call a good letter. Fine grammar. Perfect spelling. And look at the construction of those sentences! I take my hat off to Huey Hill of Louisville and wish him the best of luck in his most worthy effort. If I **am** thrown out on my ear, it'll serve me right. I've been getting away with this drivel for 23 years now and it's high time somebody did something about it. Just don't throw me in prison; that's all I ask. I hate prison life. I did four years at Leavenworth for selling Serutan to a man under the age of 35, and that's all I want of THAT kind of life.

* * *

The only worse fate I can think of would be to serve a year in the infantry. Friend of mine, Charley Oma, of Tacoma, Oklahoma, did a year in the Rainbow division and came out 6 inches taller than he went in. Callouses!

* * *

One letter came through with a compliment. It was from a nice old lady motorcyclist who is distantly related to the author of Uncle Tom's Cabin and who recently finished a stretch at the Atlanta Reformatory for horse-whipping her better half. Her name is Harriet Beecher Huzz-band. She writes: "I love your column, Bobby. If only you could talk or sing to us readers instead of just write. The printed page is so lifeless. Couldn't you persuade your editor to give away a phonograph record of you singing a song, with every copy of *The Motorcyclist*? And would you sing, just for me, that very popular song about the butcher who's inspecting his butcher shop tools ... you know the one ... 'I'm Looking Over a Four Loaf Cleaver,' or something like that?"

* * *

Well, our editor tells me this is impossible but if enough readers will demand it, he'll send me on a personal appearance tour all over the United States, Hindustan and Nicaragua and let me sing all I want to. I really hope something can be done toward this end as I've always wanted to travel and all my friends want me to travel, too.

* * *

I'd especially like to visit Hindustan. I have an uncle over there who's a whirling dervish, and is tops in his profession. Only recently he won an international competition with 916 r.p.m.

On his evening sports program "Strictly Sports," Dad made lots of predictions and would sometimes follow a "Yale over Dartmouth" with a few extra like Moon over Miami, Eggs over Easy or Man over Board. With listeners like author/humorist and Connecticut resident James Thurber writing to him to offer additional puns, his word play continued to be better than his notorious predictions. Dad also occasionally wrote guest sports columns for Connecticut dailies. This one, in October, 1947 filled in for Samuel B. Cohen of the Meriden Journal.

SAYINGS *of the* SPECTATOR

By SAMUEL B. COHEN

BY BOB STEELE
Sportscaster
Radio Station WTIC

Howdy, sports fans, and everybody! Hawaii tonight? Or is it morning? I'm never sure just what part of the day it is, what with getting up so early I'm having lunch when the rest of the world is eating breakfast, or having dinner when others are straightening out the lettuce in their sandwiches.

Now, before I go deeper into this column, perhaps I should explain how the heck I got in here, anyway. It seems that my esteemed friend, Sam Cohen (inventor of the esteem locomotive, as everyone knows) invited me to dash off a few lines anent my experiences at the sports microphone.

(Remind me to look up that word "anent" some time.

I know it means something because I've seen it in print. Maybe it was a date line on a foreign dispatch. I don't know.)

Well, I've interviewed some five hundred celebrities in eleven years at WTIC, but I think the most memorable one was Sandor Szabo. Szabo, by the way, is easy to pronounce. If you have a Southern accent say "Garbo," it rhymes with that. No, on second thought, it wasn't Szabo, either. It was a character called the "The Polish Giant," a rassler whose real name I can't recall. And it's a good thing, too, because I couldn't spell it.

It was a Winter's night and I had gone on the air with "Strictly Sports" with very little material.

I had been promised an interview with this behemoth of the mat but he hadn't shown up at the appointed time.

Air-time came. I gave my usual opening. But, from that point, I knew not where to go. Desperate, I decided to talk about professional wrestling.

Bitter to the core, I began a diatribe on the "sport" of wrestling that surprised even myself. I was so incensed that I belched out a harangue that must have smoked as it came out of loudspeakers. I accused all mat performers of being fakes and said the only thing about the game that was on the level was the ring—and even that was tilted a bit.

Then, out of words, I stopped to ponder some other subject I knew well enough to ad lib a few words on. Before I could open my mouth on Motorcycle Racing (which I always fall back on in time of stress) a bald-headed man twice my size and wearing a size 19 collar (at least) walked past me and sat down quietly. He said nothing. Neither did I.

Then a second figure passed my chair, sat down beside the other, and also stared into my blinking eyes. This second bird was the Polish Giant! I'll swear the man was seven feet tall SITTING DOWN! His companion, I deduced, was Stanislaus Zybysko. One of the great wrestlers of another day, Zybysko was managing the Giant.

I realized they had been listening to my tirade. Needless to say, I expected any second to be sailing through the air, through the studio door, and into the corridor on the end of a flying mare, or to find myself at least one-quarter or five-sixteenths mangled by a half-nelson. I remained at my post but only under the greatest stress.

For the balance of the program—some six terrible minutes—I interviewed Zybysko, speaking of his chosen profession in the most glowing terms and heaping praise on the sport of wrestling until my words almost fell over each other and crashed to the floor.

Occasionally I directed a question at The Giant, but he'd only grunt. I was convinced he was trying to decide whether he'd tie me in a sailor's knot or just plain bash my head against the wall.

Finally the time came to sign off and I clutched my throat and edged toward the door. But before I could reach it, my two guests were upon me. Zybysko shot out his huge right hand and The Giant slapped an enormous left mitt on my shoulder and—both broke into smiles and shook my hand and patted me on the back!

Zybysko just wanted to tell me how happy he was to have a mention of his coming world champion "over such a great and powerful station as WTIC!"

He said to me, winking, "We both heard your remarks but only I understood. He doesn't savvy a word of English and you can bet I'll never tell what you said. As for me, Bob, I've heard that stuff before and got used to it long since!"

A piece Dad wrote in 1944 was a longer and quite serious Popping of the Day, though, as usual, not without its humor, and he sent it to the Hartford <u>Times</u> instead of <u>The Motorcyclist</u>. It was published September 12, 1944. That was about a year after he began doing the morning program on WTIC where The Word for the Day formally began.

Air Waves Bumpy

Pronouncing Place Names No 'Czinch'

By Bob Steele

Not being a professor, or even a college man, I suppose I have no right to bat out an article on the pronunciation of proper names. However, I can claim to be a radio announcer who has been educated the hard way these past eight years at WTIC.

I have found it impossible to pronounce any name in any manner without getting at least a dozen letters telling me to give up and go back to Missouri, where it so happens, I came from. If I say Vittorio Emanuele with proper Italian treatment, listeners say, "Why don't you come down to earth, with the rest of us, and say Victor Emanuel?" If I say Victor Emanuel they ask if I also say Jorjuz Cluh-menso for Georges Clemenceau. They want to know what I'm doing on the radio if I can't handle foreign names as they're supposed to be handled.

So you see it's a pretty ticklish business, this going on the air with a newscast or a commentary on a program of classical music, while perhaps a million pairs of ears are lying in ambush, ready to twitch at the first sound that doesn't come in on them for a three-point landing. When I pronounce a French name such as Belfort without sounding the "t," the particular group whose ears zig-zag at this one want to know why I'm not consistent. They point out that I say Paris, not Paree. And that starts an argument in which I fight for my announcing life. As a matter of fact, it started me on my way to this very typewriter.

Consistency Impossible

My contention is that it's ridiculous to try to be consistent. Of course I say Paris. And I pronounce Rheims the American way: Reemz, not Ranss with a nasal "n." Those are just a couple of French names that have become so common to us in their American version that to give them the French costume would be to make them virtually unrecognizable.

I believe radio should be as clear as possible without being juvenile. If the listener misses a portion of a sentence he is apt to lose the thought and he can't go back and retrace the words, as he can do with a sentence in radio's competitor, the newspaper. So, why should I nasalize the end of a short name, like Rheims or Hams and make it unintelligible to those who know nothing about the language? Yet, there are many French words that I can pronounce in that tongue without endangering the message. These are some that I say as L'Homme Francais does: Limoges, Ypres, Poitiers. Now I think I'm justified in not Americanizing these and their kind. Could I say Ly-mo-juz? Wiperz? (By the way, how are the windshield ypres on your car?), Poy-teerz? No! I feel as well as know that Lee-mozh, Eepr', Pwah-tyay are pronunciations to give. My proposition is: Walk the fence. Don't attempt to be consistent. You can't be, and live with yourself. Let your conscience guide you.

Come and Try It

To those who say we should come down to earth and Americanize every foreign name and word, I issue the cordial invitation to come to my house and work out some good old, homey, American pronunciations for Przemysi (Poland), Pszczyna (Polish Silesia), Llwchwr (Wales), Soerabaja (Java) and a few hundred others that I come in contact with in reading news of the world.

I might add that the seemingly undecipherable and unholy four clots of letters just mentioned are amazingly easy to say when spoken in the native tongue: Pshem-ishl, Psh-chee-na, Look-er and Soo-ra-by-a. My feeling is that giving foreign pronunciations the correct way (especially when they're this easy to enunciate) will eventually bring even the non-linguist around to using them and everyone will be happy. If we Americans can say such words and place names as rendezvous, cliche, Mackinac, La Jolla, San Jose, Spuyten Duyvil and so on, then eventually, we can pronounce Villers-Bocage, Perigueux and all the rest correctly. How to know the exception when we see it will have to rest with our judgment.

Just let's remember to walk the fence a bit, bearing in mind that to try to be totally consistent is bound to get us in jams that won't wash off so easily as the kind mother puts up for winter. And now, excuse me, please. I have a newscast coming up in three minutes and so that I'll make half my audience mad and the other half glad, I must look up and learn to say two little beauties: Kangerdlugsuatsiak Fiord (Greenland) and Srivilliputtur (India).

P.S.—You'll find 'em in Webster's New International, unabridged, if you're the curious, courageous type.

Those who've been listening to Bob Steele for even a few of the past 65 years know that his wit comes across even better when he has a live audience. His distinctive baritone, his avuncular style, and his exquisite sense of timing in telling a joke or spinning a yarn are what we remember best. Tellingly, listeners frequently speak of their frustration in trying to retell a joke or a story he told that had made them laugh out loud, only to find that it somehow fell flat upon the retelling.

When Dad began doing public-address announcing for motorcycle races in California during the Depression, his love of words and good fun really found its voice. The craft of reaching an audience by talking into a microphone brought him, a few years later, to Hartford, where, we all know, it found its true home.

PRONUNCIATION KEY

       We've tried to make it easy to figure out our phonetic key for
how each entry is pronounced or mispronounced. Our pronunciation
key avoids inverted *e*'s, double-dotted *a*'s and the like. Our system may
be over-simplified in spots, but we think that's a small price to pay for
ease of use. Although the pronunciation of some syllables can be represented phonetically by simple words they sound like, we stick to our
Pronunciation Key, then note rhymes or similar sounds in parentheses.
For example, Bryn Mawr: brin MAHR (MAHR sounds like *mar*).
Don't say: brin MOR (MOR rhymes with *for*).

a	adulation, abacus, fat, parrot
ah	pa, father, Bach, Chicago, alms, top
ahr	arc, arbiter, bar, harm
ai	fair, dare, pear, where, ale, wail
ay	may, state, base, labor
aw	jaw, hawk, lawn, all, cause, thought
e	set, elm, pep, rest
ee	tree, neat, money, abalone
eer	dear, deer, pier, here
i, ih	it, pin, lip, six, sick, schism
	(short *i* is designated by *ih* and by *i* before consonants)
igh, y	my, wine, eye, tie, sight, size, aisle
o, oh	go, row, sew, coat, phone
oo	do, rude, food, pool, cruel, rue, brew
or	nor, more, war, four, door, torn
oor	poor, lure, cure, tour, endure
ow	how, power, trout, down, towel
oy	boy, toil, envoy, turquoise
u	good, stood, would, wool, pull
uh	up, around, abacus, come, thumb
ul	lull, bulk, essential, residential
ull	pull, Pulitzer, full, wool, beautiful
ur	fur, fir, earn, were, prefer
us	bus, fuss, trust, abacus, glorious

ch	which, witch, teach, chore

'l	abominable, channel, dismantle
'm	bosom, album, chasm, prism
'n	open, fatten, season, Groton, forbidden
'r	letter, sweater, debtor, accelerator

hw	whale, whisper, whet
j	jam, major, age, allege, educate, ridge
k	kit, corn, access, pick
ng	ring, song
s	sea, abacus, accelerator
sh	ship, wash, nation, precious, conscious
th	thin, path, Smith or this, weather, writhe (see entry)
z	zoo, dozen, phase
zh	vision, pleasure, casualty, prestige, massage

We indicate stress with capital letters, and when two syllables of a word are stressed, we indicate the greater stress in **BOLDFACED** capital letters. For example, *academia* is rendered phonetically: AK-uh-**DEE**-mee-uh.

When we give alternative pronunciations, we put our preferred pronunciation first. When we introduce an alternative pronunciation with "Also:", we mean to say not merely that we don't prefer it but that we regard it as less acceptable. If you'd like a much more scholarly discussion of pronunciation than what we have attempted here, including the etymology behind pronunciation and the variations among dictionaries, we highly recommend Charles Harrington Elster's *The Big Book of Beastly Mispronunciations*. (Houghton Mifflin, 1999)

a Many experts have warned against pronouncing this article *ay* instead of *uh* except for emphasis, but we think it really comes down to diction, context and personal style more than anything else. Radio and television announcers and other public speakers have a tendency to use the long *a* at times simply because it suits the rhythm and sound they unconsciously want in a phrase or sentence. (That's *uh* phrase.)

a.m. in the morning when you need to distinguish from a.m. in the afternoon. See: **amplitude modulation**

abacus AB-uh-kus (kus sounds like *cuss*)
Also: uh-BAK-us (BAK sounds like *back*)
They may not be able to use an abacus, but if you think dogs can't count just let Fido see you put three biscuits in your pocket and then try to give him just two.

abalone ab-uh-LOH-nee
Definition: a shellfish used for food and ornament

aberrant uh-BAIR-unt or ab-AIR-unt
Also: AB-uhr-unt
Definition: deviating from the usual; abnormal
Wife says to husband, "What's the idea of coming home half-drunk?" He answers, "I ran out of money."

abominable uh-BAHM-in-uh-b'l

It's always tempting to simplify and shorten, but that's a poor excuse for uh-BAHM-nih-b'l. There are five syllables in this word. Don't leave the *i* out.

My Uncle Corrugated says the town where he lives is abominable. Just the other night at 3 a.m. someone was pounding and screaming at his door. But he ignored them and went on quietly playing his bagpipe.

abscond ab-SKAHND

Don't say: ab-SKOUND

However, one who absconds might be called an abscoundrel.

absentia See: in absentia

absurd ab-SURD (SURD rhymes with *third*)

Don't say: ab-ZURD

Note, too, that *absorb* is ab-SORB, not ab-ZORB. The preferred pronunciation of *absolve*, however, is ab-ZOLVE, not ab-SOLVE.

academia AK-uh-**DEE**-mee-uh
(rhymes with *Bohemia*) (AK as in *sack*)
Don't say:
AK-uh-**DAY**-mee-uh or AK-uh-**DEM**-ee-uh

Thinking of *academe* (AK-uh-deem) may help to
pronounce academia correctly.
*A grade schooler was having a rough time with
his homework. Finally he asked his mother if she'd
do it for him, and she objected: "It wouldn't be
right." The boy responded, "But gee, Mom, you
could at least try."*

academician AK-uh-duh-**MISH**-'n or
uh-KAD-uh-**MISH**-'n (AK as in *sack*)

Acapulco AK-uh-**PULL**-ko (AK as in *sack*)
Don't say: AL-kuh-**PULL**-ko

Al Capone may have vacationed there, or gone
for a working vacation, but there's only one *l* in
Acapulco.

accede ak-SEED (ak as in *sack*)
Don't say: uh-SEED

Where you have a double *c*, you're going to get a
k sound. Thus *recede*, but *succeed*. See: **accessory**
and **accelerator**.

accelerator ak-SEL-uh-ray-t'r (ak as in *sack*)
Don't say: uh-SEL-uh-ray-t'r
See: **accessory, flaccid, succinct**

accessory ak-SES-uh-ree (ak as in *sack*)
Don't say: uh-SES-uh-ree
See: **accelerator, flaccid, succinct**. The first *c* in
cce or *cci* has a *k* sound, the second an *s* sound.

No one seems to have any trouble with *vaccina-tion or succeed*, though some worry over *accept* and *accede*.

In words with double C's, express
C first as K, then as S:
A*k*-SEPT, a*k*-SEDE, a*k*-SESS-ory.
One time there was a silly lout
Who always left the K sound out.
He said a*ss*-EPT, he said su*ss*-INCT;
He luckily became extinct
Before he could propose that we
Reverse the sounds of double C
And say a*ss*-KEPT, a*ss*-KESS-ory.

WILLIAM R. ESPY

acclimate AK-lih-mayt (AK as in *sack*) or uh-KLY-mayt

accommodate uh-KAHM-ih-dayt
Just remember that *accommodate* contains all the *c*'s and *m*'s it can accommodate.

accompanist uh-KUHM-puh-nist
Don't say: uh-KUHM-puh-nee-ist
The verb *accompany* fools many into wanting to add an extra *i* in *accompanist*. Don't be fooled. It's not *accompaniist*.

accouterment, accoutrement uh-KOO-tur-mint
Don't say: uh-KOO-truh-mint
There are two spellings for this fancy word for clothing accessories, but only one pronunciation.

acerbic uh-SURB-ik
A single *c* followed by an *e* or *i* (e.g. *acid*) usually takes the *s* sound. Otherwise expect a *k* sound: *acolyte*, *acrid*, **actual**, **acumen**.

acropolis uh-CRAHP-'l-is (CRAHP sounds like *crop*)
Watch out for: uh-CRAHP-lis

activity Beware using *activity* when you don't need it. Why, for example, do weatherforecasters have to predict "major thunderstorm activity" when predicting "major thunderstorms" would do quite nicely?

actor AK-t'r
Don't say: AK-tor (rhymes with *back door*)
See: **factor**

actual AK-choo-'l
Don't say: AK-sh'l

acumen uh-KYOO-m'n
Not as good: AK-yuh-men

adage AD-ij
Don't say: uh-DAYJ or AD-ayj

adieu uh-DYOO or uh-DOO
Don't confuse *adieu*, which means the act of taking one's leave with *ado*, which means bustle or fuss.

When I was a kid in Kansas City I had two dogs. Their names were Fail, a German Shepard, and Further Ado, a poodle. I like odd names for dogs. Everybody seems to name their dogs Rex and Trixie and so on. I'll never forget how my Aunt Josephine, who lived in Rich Hill, about a hundred miles south, would invite me down every once in a while, but she didn't like dogs. So she would say, "Now, please come down next weekend without Fail and without Further Ado."

adjective   A-jik-tiv or AJ-ik-tiv
The *d* is silent, as it is in *adjoin, adjudicate, adjunct, adjust, adjure* and *adjutant*. And see: **adulation.**
A-juh-tiv, though often heard, is sloppy.

admirable   AD-m'-ruh-b'l
Few people have a problem putting the accent on the first syllable of *admirable*, so let it be an example for the adjectives *applicable, comparable, formidable, lamentable* and *preferable*. Putting the stress on the first syllable in words of three or more syllables is easier if you're used to it, as words like *admirable, actual* and *adjective* show.

adrenal   uh-DREE-n'l
Don't say: uh-DRE-n'l

adrenaline,   uh-DREN-'l-'n (for either spelling)
adrenalin   Avoid: uh-DREN-'l-een

adulation AJ-uh-**LAY**-shun
Don't say: AD-yoo-**LAY**-shun.
See: **arduous**

adult uh-DULT
Not preferred: ad-ULT

A teenager went to his father and said, "Dad,
don't you think it's time I stood on my own two
feet? Don't you think I should face the world
and handle my own problems?"
His father said, proudly, "Yes, son, I do."
The kid said, "Well, I can't do it on the allowance
I get now."

adverse, averse The fact that these words sound so much alike is
no doubt the reason they're so often confused. We
might hear, for example, "She is not adverse to
compliments on her cooking." The speaker should
have said *averse*. Both words suggest a negative
notion but *adverse* is stronger, suggesting antago-
nism, and is more appropriate for describing
things than people. "He was bothered by the
adverse comments about his cooking."

advertisement AD-ver-**TYZ**-ment
British: ad-VUR-tiz-ment or ad-VUR-tis-ment
*An ad-VUR-tiz-ment over a butcher shop in
London proclaims proudly: "We make sausage for
Queen Elizabeth." Above a rival shop across the
street is another sign: "God save the Queen."*

advocate (noun) AD-vuh-kit
(verb) AD-vuh-kayt
The pattern of words ending in *ate* to take the *it*
pronunciation as nouns or adjectives and the *ate*
pronunciation as verbs can be found in *aggregate*,

alternate, animate, appropriate, approximate, associate, delegate, degenerate, duplicate, elaborate, estimate, graduate, incarnate, initiate, moderate, precipitate, separate, subordinate and *syndicate,* among others. But the preferred pronunciation for **candidate** (a noun only, never an adjective or a verb), is KAN-d'-dayt.

I was born Robert Jesse Steele, July 13, 1911 in Kansas City, Missouri, when the U.S. still had just 46 states.

Aegean igh-JEE-'n (igh sounds like *eye*).
Don't say: i-EE-jin

aegis EE-jis
Don't say: AY-jis or IGH-jis (IGH sounds like *eye*)
Definition: sponsorship or protection

The *ae* is a "ligature" from Latin pronounced *ee* in a number of words, including:

> *Aesop*
> *algae*
> *alumnae*
> *antennae*
> *archaeology*
> *athenaeum*
> *formulae*
> *larvae*
> *minutiae*
> *vertebrae*

affect, effect These words are easily confused in part because they sound so much alike when used as verbs. To *affect* is to influence; to *effect* is to bring about. A result is not an affect but an effect. Many improperly use *effect* as a verb when they mean *affect*. When *affect* refers to a person's facial expression or emotion, it's pronounced A-fekt.

affiant uh-FEE-unt
Avoid: AF-ee-unt
Definition: one who swears to an affidavit

affluent, affluence AF-loo-int, AF-loo-ints
Don't say: uh-FLOO-'nt, uh-FLOO-'nts

aged a-j'd – as a noun: She lived in a home for the aged.

ayjd – as the past participle of the verb "to age": He aged years in a few months.

An officer who pulled a motorist to the side of the road exclaimed, "When I saw you come zooming around that curve, I said to myself, 55 at least!" "Well, you're wrong, officer," protested the woman. "This hat just makes me look older."

I used an even more dated variant of this joke in a 1936 "Prof. Popper" column I wrote for many years for the monthly magazine *The Motorcyclist*: "I picked up the special Ladies' Edition of *The Motorcyclist*...and I want to hand the 'weaker' sex a lot of credit. Never knew they were so active in the sport that used to belong to men. That issue certainly put 'em on the map and you can figure on having your cylinders reground and a new paint job on the old crock by a feminine hand in another few years. The wimmin can tackle just about any job nowadays but a woman will never be the president of the United States. The Constitution says a person must be 35 years of age to be eligible for that office."

agglutination the formation of new words by combining other words or parts of words.

OPERATOR
OF
BEAUTY SALON
BEAUTY SHOPERATOR

balloonatic	person crazy about balloons
disastrophe	disaster-catastrophe
eggzibbit	display at a poultry show
grismal	grim-dismal
hoptician	one who prescribes spectacles for rabbits, kangaroos or frogs
hurrycane	walking stick for a fast-paced grandpa
Lostralian	a Digger who disappears in the Outback
parkatect	city landscape designer
Ohareport	O'Hare Airport
scrubmarine	boat for cleaning the ocean floor
snorekeeper	scientist who records sleeping habits
talcaholic	one who overuses bath powder
thunderwriter	insurance professional who determines storm risk coverage
zooperintendent	superintendent of a zoo

This is our contribution to the energy crisis. Think of all the ink and paper these innovations could save! It's not a lot, but it's more than the contribution of my neighbor. He saves energy by sleeping a half hour later every morning.

aggrandize uh-GRAN-dighz or AG-run-dighz

aggravate Definition: to make worse. The use of *aggravate* to mean annoy or irritate is common but poor usage.

albeit awl-BEE-it
This word, meaning "even though," looks like awl-BIGHT (BIGHT like *bite*). Don't say: awl-BIGHT, al-BEE-it or al-bee-IT.

alleged uh-LEJD (rhymes with *edged*)
Don't say: uh-LEJ-id, whether using it as a verb or an adjective.

The two syllables of *alleged* become three when the suffix *ly* is added to make the four-syllable adverb *allegedly*, fooling many into pronouncing the adjective uh-LEJ-id. *Alleged* sounds like *edged*, *dredged* and *full-fledged* (and *half-fledged*, for that matter). It's like **marked** or **supposed** but not like *one-legged*, *barelegged*, *bareheaded* or *right-handed*, or like **beloved**, which can be pronounced with either two or three syllables.

The temptation to give three syllables to *alleged* may also come from the change some nouns may undergo after being used as verbs in the past tense, if then used as adjectives or changed back into nouns. The man *aged* (ayjd) years in a few weeks, but he lives in a home for the *aged* (a-j'd). They *winged* (wingd) their way home on a 747 after seeing the *Winged* Victory (wing-id or wingd) at the Louvre. See **iced tea**.

allies   AL-yz (yz sounds like *eyes*)
Not as good: uh-LYZ

alma mater   AWL-muh MAHT-ur (AWL sounds like *all*)
Don't say: AL-muh MAHT-ur

almond   AH-mund or AHM-und
Also: AHL-mund (AHL as in *doll*) or AWL-mund

alms   ahms
Don't say: *alms*
The *l* is silent as in *balm*, *calm*, *palm*, *psalm* and *qualm*.

already   awl-RED-ee
Already provides a good example of the flexibility of pronunciation to fit a speaker's cadence, rhythm, meter. In this sentence, combined with another expression, it may be legitimately pronounced AWL-red-ee: "An already-burned-out house greeted the marauding predators."

alright   This word is not all right, not okay. It's not like *already*. Use two words, all right? As someone once said, "*Alright* is always and altogether all wrong."

alumnae   uh-LUM-nee
Definition: female graduates of a school. *Alumnae* is the plural of *alumna*. *Alumnus*, a male graduate, takes the plural form *alumni* (uh-LUM-nigh). *Alumni* can also refer to all the graduates of a coeducational school.

Alzheimer's   AHLTS-high-murz
This word is commonly pronounced and mispronounced so many different ways that you can't be blamed if you think anything goes. But not all

pronunciations are created equal.
Okay: ALTS-high-murz (ALT as in *shalt*)
Less okay: AWLZ-high-murz
Not okay: ALZ-high-murz (ALZ sounds like *Al*'s)

amateur AM-uh-tur
Second best: AM-uh-chur
Worst: AM-uh-chyoor
Beyond description: AM-uh-tyoor

See: **connoisseur, entrepreneur** and other words from the French ending in *eur*: **saboteur, auteur, raconteur, chauffeur, provocateur, restaurateur, hauteur, liqueur, de rigeur, voyeur**

amazed, surprised Finding her husband with another woman, she cried, "I'm surprised at you!" "No, he replied, "I'm surprised — you're amazed."

ambassador am-BAS-uh-dur
Don't say: am-**BAS**-uh-DOR

ambergris AM-b'r-grees or AM-b'r-gris
The *s* is not silent.

Definition: a substance derived from the intestines of sperm whales and used in some perfumes. Upon noting the origins of this prized substance, *Moby Dick*'s Ishmael commented, "Who would think, then, that such fine ladies and gentlemen should regale themselves with an essence found in the inglorious bowels of a sick whale!"

ambiance, ambience AM-bee-ents
Also: AM-bee-ints and AM-bee-ahnts

Not an Italian or French designer. This is an anglicized word that may always feel as if it's still French, leading speakers to want to make it sound a little, though hardly ever entirely, French.

ambidextrous am-bih-DEX-strus

Don't say: am-bih-DEX-tur-us

Yogi Berra is reputed to have said of a ballplayer, "He hits from both sides of the plate. He's amphibious."

amen AY-**MEN** or AH-**MEN**

The rounder, softer *a* being more musical, easier on the ear, AH-MEN is more commonly heard in the singing of hymns.

"E. W. Howe tells a story of a little girl in Kansas whose mother, on acquiring social aspirations, entered the Protestant Episcopal Church from the Methodist Church. The father remaining behind, the little girl had to learn to say *amen* with the *a* of *rake* when she went to church with her father and *amen* with the *a* of *car* when she went to church with her mother."

H. L. MENCKEN, *The American Language*

amenable uh-MEE-nuh-b'l or uh-MEN-uh-b'l

amenity uh-MEN-ih-tee or uh-MEE-nih-tee

Amherst Am-urst

Don't say: AM-hurst

The *h* is silent, for Amherst, MA; Amherst, NY; Amherst College and Lord Jeffrey Amherst, an English general and governor of British North America who fought the French in the 1760s.

Back in 1978 I got a letter from John Coolidge of Plymouth, Vermont, son of President Calvin Coolidge. He wrote, "A few weeks ago you mentioned that although my father was known as 'Silent Cal' he was the class orator upon the occasion of his graduation from Amherst College in 1895. Actually, he was the Grove Orator. The

Grove Oration is a humorous dissertation poking fun at one's classmates. Father always had a good sense of humour. You may recall he is the only U.S. President born on July 4th (1872)." Note that even in 1978 the British spelling of *humor* was still around, at least in Vermont.

amicable   AM-uh-kuh-b'l
Don't say: uh-MEEK-uh-b'l

amicus curiae   uh-MIGHK-us KYOOR-ih-ee
Definition: friend of the court; someone, not a party to litigation, who volunteers advice to the court. A legal term. Outside the law, the term is busybody.

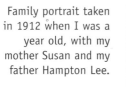

Family portrait taken in 1912 when I was a year old, with my mother Susan and my father Hampton Lee.

Amish   AH-mish
Less common: AM-ish

ammonia   uh-MOHN-yuh or uh-MOHN-ee-uh

amok, amuck   uh-MUK
(same pronunciation with either spelling)

amplitude modulation My 65 years on the radio have all been on WTIC-A.M. 1080 in Hartford, Connecticut, U.S.A. A.M. stands for amplitude modulation, a system for radio broadcasting by a method of impressing a signal on a radio carrier wave by varying its width. I have no idea what that means.

For many years WTIC's clear channel signal could sometimes be picked up all over the world, and I would occasionally get letters from far-off places. In fact, I got several from Sydney Australia. Mr. Australia lives in Bridgeport. Over the years, as more stations filled the airwaves, WTIC's signal no longer reached other continents, and even Boston became a stretch. In 1953, Archibald MacLeish, the poet, playwright, FDR speechwriter and Librarian of Congress, who had occasionally written to me from Western Massacusetts, wrote: "My one serious complaint about Cambridge (I am now teaching at Harvard) is that I can't hear you while I shave."

analog, analogue Different spelling, same pronunciation. That applies likewise to *catalog* and *catalogue; dialog* and *dialogue, monolog* and *monologue*. Except for the name of a computer program, we've never seen the spelling of *prologue* shortened to *prolog*.

analogous uh-NAL-uh-gus
Don't say: uh-NAL-uh-jus
Since *analogy* is pronounced uh-NAL-uh-jee rather than uh-NAL-uh-gee, the pronunciations of *analogous* and *analogy* are not analogous. The *g* in *analogous* is like the *g* in *analogue*.

anarchy AN-ur-kee
Don't say: AN-AHR-kee or an-AHR-kee
See: **monarchy**

ancillary AN-suh-lair-ee
British: an-SILL-uh-ree

and so The *and* is redundant, or the *so* is. Both are conjunctions and add very little, if anything, by being joined. There's nothing wrong, though, with the expressions *and so on* or *and so forth*.

anemone uh-NEM-uh-nee
Don't say: AN-uh-moan
It's tempting to pronounce the first two letters of *anemone* as a unit, as in *animal* or *anemometer* (an instrument for measuring wind speed). Also watch out for confusing the *n* and *m*, as some children will do with *animal*. One of my grandsons, at the age of 10, was still saying *aminal*.

angina pectoris an-JIGH-nuh or AN-jih-nuh PEK-tur-is
Avoid: pek-TOR-is

angst ANKST or AHNKST

annual No event should be called "first annual," except in hindsight. The First Styrofoam Art Festival, for example, isn't an annual event until and unless a Second Annual Styrofoam Art Festival takes place.

annul uh-NUL

antarctic ant-AHRK-tik
Don't say: ant-AHR-tik or an-AHR-tik
Don't miss the *c* or the first *t*! See: **arctic.**
The Antarctic, by the way, capitalized, means the continent of Antarctica and the Antarctic Ocean around it.

antennae an-TEN-ee
Don't say: an-TEN-igh (igh as in *high*)

anti- AN-tee
Avoid: an-TIGH. This prefix is pronounced AN-tee in most words, but AN-tih in a few such as *antidote*.

The prefix **semi-** also takes the long *i* with emphasis on the first syllable: SEM-ee, not SEM-igh. See: **quasi-**

Shakespeare notwithstanding, a Jesse by any other name would be a lot sweeter to me! When I was 6, I disliked a neighborhood bully by the name of Jesse so much that I persuaded my mother to drop my middle name in favor of Lee, my father's middle name. In 1944 I passed it on to Philip Lee.

antidote AN-tih-doht
An antidote is a medicine taken to prevent dotes.

anyways *Anyways, anywheres, nowheres* and *somewheres* are nonstandard words used by illiterate or uneducated people, or by careless educated people. Leave off the *s*. An unnecessary *s* also creeps into expressions such as *a good ways off* and *one-upsmanship*.

apartheid uh-PART-hyt (hyt like *height*) or
uh-PART-hayt (hayt like *hate*)
Don't say: uh-PAR-thyd or uh-PAR-tyd

aplomb uh-PLAHM or uh-PLUM

Oscar Wilde demonstrated great aplomb when, at the age of 16, he was invited to a formal ball in Dublin. In the course of the evening he asked one of the titled ladies of the city to dance. She looked at him coldly and said, "Do you think that I'm going to dance with a child?" Wilde replied, "Dear lady, if I had known you were in that condition, I would never have asked you to dance."

apogee **AP**-uh-JEE

Definition: highest or furthest point

Appalachia AP-uh-**LAY**-chee-uh, AP-uh-**LATCH**-ee-uh, AP-uh-**LAY**-chuh

Also: AP-uh-**LAY**-shee-uh, AP-uh-**LASH**-ee-uh, AP-uh-**LAY**-shuh

appellant uh-PEL-'nt

Don't say: uh-pel-ANT

The party against whom an appeal is taken the appellee, has the choice of AP-uh-**LEE** or uh-PEL-**EE**.

applicable AP-lih-kuh-b'l

Don't say: uh-PLIK-uh-b'l
See: **admirable**

apricot AY-prih-kaht or AP-rih-kaht

aquifer AK-wih-fur or AH-quih-fur

Arab AIR-ub

Don't say: AY-rab

arbiter AHR-bit-'r

Don't say: AHR-byt-ur

An AHR-bit-'r is one who decides arguments, an umpire. An AHR-byt-ur is a tester in an alphabet soup factory.

archetype AHR-kih-typ (typ sounds like *type*).
Don't say: ARCH-typ

Definition: original or basic pattern or model

archfiend ARCH-FEEND

Definition: number one fiend, a devil

Where *arch* is part of a compound word it takes the *ch* sound as in *archbishop, archdiocese, archduke, archenemy, archway.* There is one exception, *archangel*, where the *ch* takes a *k* sound. The *k* sound is the rule where the word is not a compound, as in *archaeology, archaic, architecture, archive, Archimedes.* There is an exception to this rule too: *archer, archery.*

archipelago AHR-kih-**PEL**-uh-go
Don't say: ARCH-ih-**PEL**-uh-go

archive, AHR-kyv (kyv rhymes with *dive* and *jive*),
archivist AHRK-ih-**VIST**
Don't say: AR-chyv (chyv sounds like *chive*) or
ahr-KIGH-vist

arctic ARK-tik
Don't say: AR-tik

We won't complain though if you call your
galoshes AR-tiks. When Phil was a kid, we called
them galoshes. One day when it came time to
come home from school, Phil's teacher had to help
all her pupils into their galoshes. After pulling and
tugging on 30 pairs, she came to Phil. When she
had finally gotten his galoshes on him, he said,
"You know, teacher, these aren't mine."

arduous AHR-joo-us or ARDGE-yoo-us
Don't say: AHRD-yoo-us

DON'T BE
AFRAID
TO SAY----

EDUCATE   TIE BAR
FORTUNE

The *u* following the *d* in this word changes the *d*
so that it can't be ARD-yoo-us. The *d* takes a *j*
sound. The link between the *d* and the *u* is called
a tie bar. The same kind of thing happens in *for-tune*. The *u* changes the *t* to a *ch*, FOR-choon.
See: **assiduous**. The letter *u* doesn't always have
this effect on *d* and *t*, of course. *Fortuitous* is not
for-CHOO-ih-tus, but for-TOO-ih-tus. And while
educate is EJ-yoo-kate, *educe* is not ee-JOOS and
enduring is not en-JYOOR-ing. See: **egregious**

argot AHR-go or AHR-gut

Arkansas AHR-kan-saw

But if you're talking about the Arkansas River, you may say AHR-kan-saw or ar-KAN-z's, depending especially on which part of the river you happen to be around. See: **Missouri**

armistice **AHRM**-ih-STIS
Don't say: ahr-MIS-tis

arteriosclerosis ahr-TEER-ee-o-skluh-**ROH**-sis
Long words are a lot easier to say if you think of them as two or more words: *arterio sclerosis*. You can try out this suggestion on Lake Chargoggagoggmanchaugagogchaubunagungga-maug. See: **Indian**

arthritis ahr-THRY-tis
Don't say: AHR-thur-I-tis
Two elderly ladies met, and one said to the other: What do you do with your time all day?" Her friend's reply was, "Oh, my men friends take up all of my day. I have breakfast with CHARLIE-horse; lunch with ARTHUR-itis; I dine with WILL-power, and go to bed with BEN-gay."

asbestos as-BES-tus or az-BES-tus

Ascot AS-kut
Don't say: AS-KAHT
AS-KAHT is a common mispronunciation for ascot, the scarf or necktie that takes its name from Ascot, the site of the famous annual English horse race.

asphalt AS-fawlt (fawlt sounds like *fault*)
Don't say: ASH-fawlt

aspirin   AS-prin or AS-p'-rin
Nine out of ten doctors recommend aspirin.
One prefers headaches.

assailant   uh-SAIL-'nt
Avoid: uh-SAIL-yunt

assiduous   uh-SIJ-oo-wus or uh-SIJ-oo-us
Don't say: uh-SID-yoo-us. See: **arduous**

assignee   uh-sigh-NEE or as-uh-NEE
Definition: one to whom something is assigned

associate   (noun) uh-SO-shee-it or uh-SO-see-it
(verb) uh-SO-shee-ate or uh-SO-see-ate
See: **advocate**

assuage   uh-SWAYJ
Don't say: uh-SWAHJ or uh-SWAYZH
See: **garage**

asterisk   AS-tuh-risk
Don't say: AS-tuh-rix
The *s* comes before the *k*, not after.
Asterisk is derived from aster, the Greek word
for star.

asthma   AZ-muh
Say this word, as well as **isthmus**, as if it had no
th in the middle.

I know a New Yorker who wanted to get away from the crime and violence of the City. He moved to Arizona where he was attacked by a mugger with asthma.

Asunción uh-SOON-syohn
(Paraguay) Don't say: uh-SUN-shun

atelier at-'l-YAY
Definition: a workshop or studio, especially of an artist

athenaeum, ATH-uh-**NEE**-um (for either spelling)
atheneum Don't say: ATH-uh-**NAY**-um or uh-THEE-nee-um
The great museum in Hartford is *The Wadsworth Atheneum*. Don't spell it with an *ae*.

athlete, ATH-leet, ath-LET-ix
athletics Don't say: ATH-uh-leet, ath-uh-LET-ix
Athletic ability is only one part of success in sports. Iron nerve is important too. For example, in golf, looking an opponent in the eye and saying, "That was a practice swing."
See: **biathlon, decathlon, pentathlon, triathlon**

atoll AT-awl
Also: uh-TAHL

Attila AT-ih-luh
Among those who give little care to pronunciation: uh-TILL-uh
It is so natural to talk in a rhythm approximating iambic meter (duh-DUH, duh-DUH) that second syllable emphasis is almost unavoidable for Attila in the phrase "Attila the Hun."

Audubon **AW**-duh-BAHN
Don't say: **AW**-dyoo-BAHN or **AW**-joo-BAHN

John James Audubon (1785-1851) was an American naturalist and artist famous for his drawings of birds.

aunt ahnt or ant

While *ahnt* is used in New England and much of the East, *ant* is common throughout most of the rest of the country.

Aunt Bessemer (that's Ant Bess—being from Missouri) makes a wonderful cake. She calls it sponge cake because she borrows all the ingredients.

I started boxing when I was 16. After 52 amateur bouts, I turned pro but won just two of 16 fights (I was robbed 14 times), leading me, at age 19, to retire from the profession. But my knowledge of the sport later became a valuable asset in radio broadcasting.

auxiliary awg-ZIL-yuh-ree

Don't say: awg-ZIL-uh-ree or awg-ZIL-ee-air-ee
Various organizations are always asking me to
read the strangest announcements over the air.
One from a women's auxiliary said, "Church
women have cast off clothing and may be seen
at the church basement Saturday night."

avant-garde AH-vohnt GAHRD (sounds like *guard*)
AH-vahnt GAHRD
AV-ahnt GAHRD

awry uh-RY

Don't say: AW-ree
It doesn't rhyme with *Maury* or *Laurie*.

*A guy asks, "What's wrong with me, doctor?" The
answer, "You're too fat, you smoke like a chimney,
you huff and puff, you drink too much, and you're
in the wrong office. I'm a lawyer."*

Azores AY-zorz or uh-ZORZ

B

Bach You may laugh, but before I started in radio I thought the way to say it was Batch. I also used to say BEETH-oven, BRAMS, CHOP-in and De-BUSS-ee. In those days, of course, we had fewer guides in how to say names. Nor did I care very much. Maybe as much as the price of shoe laces in twelfth century Samoa. I wasn't alone. Few people, then or now, have concerned themselves much with how to say names found in newspapers and books. Then radio came along, letting people hear these names spoken by professionals who, they assumed, knew how to pronounce them. Before radio, almost everyone called the world heavyweight champion Gene Tunney TOO-nee instead of TUN-ee. People pronounced the first syllable in the name of Teddy Roosevelt, our 26th president, like *news* or *lose*. But when FDR came along, radio made the difference in changing the pronunciation to ROSE-uh-velt.

Not knowing how to say the composers was a rough spot in my 1936 audition at WTIC. I was handed an announcement to read with a lot of six-syllable words, some I'd never seen before, much less pronounced. Instead of tackling the tongue-twisters, I sold the station manager the idea of letting me do a sports broadcast of an imaginary boxing match. I'd done it before and had it down pretty good, I thought. The manager apparently liked it. In fact, he wanted me to sign the two imaginary fighters to a return bout.

bade, forbade bad, fur-BAD

Don't say: bayd or fur-BAYD

Bade is the past tense of *bid*, as in "I bade him good-bye" and *forbade* is the past tense of *forbid*. (*Forbid* is also used for the past tense).

Marie Borroff of New Haven sent me what she titled "It Happened In Eden – A Short, Short Story"

God showed them the fruit on the bough,
And said not to touch it, no how;
If they'd done as God bade,
There'd be little to add,
But they didn't–and look at us now!

badminton BAD-min-tin

Don't say: BAD-mit-in

BAD-mit-in is often heard. It's easier to say. Why is it that the same dictionaries that recognize so many other careless mispronunciations do not recognize BAD-mit-in? Go figure.

Bahamas buh-HAH-muhz

Don't say: buh-HAY-muhz

UNCLE SAM
WANTS
ME?

RLS

balk bawk (rhymes with *hawk*, *talk* and *walk*)

Don't say: *bawlk*, just as you wouldn't say *tawlk* or *wawlk*. The *l* is silent. See: **alms, balm, caulk, calm, caulk, palm, psalm** and **qualm**.

balm　bahm (sounds like *bomb*)
Don't say: balm. The *l* is silent. See: **alms, balk, balm, calm, caulk, palm, psalm** and **qualm**

banal　BAY-n'l
Also: buh-NAHL

Bangor　BANG-gor (gor sounds like *gore*)
(Maine)　Don't say: BANG-gur

bankruptcy　BANK-rupt-see
Don't say: BANK-rup-see

People are rarely comfortable with consonant combinations except the few that blend easily such as *nt*, *st* or most of those with an *r*, and *pt* is a mouthful for the English speaker. Like FEB-yoo-air-ee for **February**, BANK-rup-see will probably become more and more common and accepted. Because the *t* feels like excess baggage or something caught between your teeth, it will probably disappear.

banquet　BANK-wit
Don't say: BAN-quit. Ban that pronunciation! Ban the *BAN*. Quit the *quit*. Say BANK-wit and you can bank on it.

baptize　BAP-tyz or bap-TYZ
There's been a tendency for centuries in English to move stress toward the first syllable. There is also a more questionable leveling tendency to regular-ize the pronunciation of noun and verb forms of words. Like most two-syllable verbs, *baptize* was

long stressed on the second syllable, but people hearing *Baptist* with its first-syllable stress, naturally tend to say BAP-tyz as well.
See: **default, increase**

barbiturate   bar-BICH-ur-it (BICH rhymes with *itch*)
Borderline: bar-BICH-ur-ayt
Borderline: bar-buh-TYOOR-it
Borderline: bar-buh-TOOR-it
No way: bar-BITCH-yoo-it

barelegged   bair-LAYG-id
Not as shapely: bare-LAYGD

Used three syllables, as you would for *bareheaded* or *barehanded*. Likewise for *two-legged*, etc. But see: **alleged**

baroque

bases   The plural of *base* is pronounced BAY-siz.
The plural of *basis* is pronounced BAY-seez.
Both plurals are spelled *bases*.

basil, basal, Basel, Basil   BAZ-'l or BAY-z'l, BAY-s'l, BAH-z'l, BA-z'l
The herb, *basil*, is pronounced BAZ-'l or BAY-z'l; *basal*, the adjective form of *base* or *basis* is BAY-s'l; *Basel*, the city in Switzerland, is BAH-z'l; and *Basil*, the man's name, is BA-z'l.

bas-relief   BAH-relief
Not an anti-depressant, but relief sculpture in which the figures stand out slightly from the background – low relief.

Bastille   ba-STEEL
It's great that France has a holiday named after me, but it's a shame they missed the date by a day. I was born July 13, 1911.

bathos   BAY-thahs (rhymes with *MS-DOS* and *Haas*, as in golfer Jay Haas) or BAY-thaws (rhymes with *sauce*).
Don't say: BATH-aws (a mispronunciation which might make you confuse the word with a place for washing) or BAY-thohs. See: **pathos, Eros, ethos** and **kudos**

beatific   bee-uh-TIF-ik
Don't say: byoo-TIF-ik

beatify, beautify   bee-AT-ih-figh, BYOO-tih-figh
(figh rhymes with *sigh*)
Don't say *beautify* (BYOO-tih-figh) if you mean *beatify* (bee-AT-ih-figh) — to declare a deceased person to be among the blessed and thus entitled to specific religious honor, to make blissfully happy. *Beautify*, of course, means to make beautiful.

beatitude be-AT-ih-tood
Don't say: BYOOT-ih-tood
Definition: supreme blessedness or happiness

beau geste boh ZHEST
Don't say: boh JEST or boh GEST

This French expression means a fine gesture, often only for show, and was the title of the 1939 film starring Gary Cooper.

beautiful BYOOT-ih-f'l
Don't say: BYOO-tee-ful

A very kind old priest was approached by a lady who told him, "Oh, Father, I believe that I have been guilty of sin every day of my life."

The kindly Father answered: "Oh, my dear lady, what makes you think that?

"Well," she replied, "Every morning when I get up and look at myself in the mirror, I tell myself how beautiful I am."

"Why, that's not a sin, my dear," the kind priest said.

"It's not?" asked the astonished lady.

"No, my dear," replied the priest. "In your case, it's simply a mistake."

behemoth bih-HEE-muhth
Also: BE-huh-mawth (mawth sounds like *moth*)

Beijing bay-JING
Don't say: bay-ZHING

Belgrade BEL-grayd
Don't say: BEL-grahd (either in Serbia or Maine)

beneficent buh-NEF-uh-sent
Don't say: BEN-uh-FISH-int

I had my first motorcycle when I was 13 and got a job selling Indian motorcycles in L.A. when I was 21. Over some 20 years of riding I probably logged over 300,000 miles. I also had many accidents, landing in the hospital 14 times. I'm 16 in this photo.

beneficiary ben-uh-FISH-ee-air-ee or ben-uh-FISH-uh-ree

Berlin bur-LIN (Germany), BUR-lin (Connecticut)

Bernard Americans mostly stress the second syllable, British the first. Former CNN anchor Bernard Shaw is bur-NARD, Irish playwright George Bernard Shaw is BUR-nurd. It was the latter who said, "England and America are two countries separated by the same language." For example, the British say luh-BOR-uh-tree for *laboratory*. They also make *schedule* sound like shed yule, and *clerk* comes out clark, *ate* is et, lever is lee-vur and *leisure* is leh-zhur. See British.

Bernstein BURN-styn or BURN-steen
The late composer Leonard Bernstein is BURN-stighn, not BURN-steen. Names should be pronounced the way their owners prefer. That's true even if the owners don't know better. Red Sox radio announcer Joe Castiglione says his name kuh-STIG-lee-ohn, even though the Italian KAS-t'-lee-OH-neh is really too beautiful to anglicize. At least he doesn't say kuh-STIG-lee-OH-nee, which some think sounds Italian. Many Americans named *Eamiello* pronounce their name ee-MEEL-ee-oh instead of ee-MYEL-oh, even

though it contradicts the spelling. NFL Commissioner Paul Tagliabue is TAG-luh-boo while his second cousin, poet John Tagliabue, who was born in Italy, pronounces his name TAHL-yah-**BOO**-eh. See: **Xavier**

besiege bih-SEEJ
Don't say: bih-SEEZH

bestial BES-chul (rhymes with *celestial* and almost with *potential*)
Don't say: BEAST-chul or BEES-tee-'l or BESH-chul
There's no *beast* in *bestial*. See: **controversial**

bestiality BES-chee-**AL**-ih-tee

betrothal bih-TROH-th'l (*th* as in *this*)
Also: bih-TRAH-th'l (*th* as in *thin*)

biathlon by-ATH-lahn (*th* as in *path*)
Watch out for: by-ATH-uh-lahn (not four syllables, but three). See: **athlete, decathlon, pentathlon** and **triathlon**

IS IT BI-SICKLE OR BI-SIGH-K'L?

SIGH! I'M SICK!

RLS

bicycle BIGH-sih-k'l
Don't say: bigh-SIGH-k'l

Bilbao (Spain) bil-BAH-oh

bilious BIL-yus (BIL rhymes with *pill*)
Don't say: BIL-ee-us
Definition: irritable; unpleasant

Biloxi bih-LUK-see (LUK sounds like *luck*)
(Mississippi) Don't say: bih-LAHK-see (LAHK sounds like *lock*)

blasphemous BLAS-fuh-mus (BLAS sounds like *glass*)
Don't say: blas-FEE-mus

blithe blyth (rhymes with *writhe* and *tithe*)
Also: blyth (th like the *th* in *Smith*—rhymes with *Smythe*)

Hawthorne's novel *The Blithedale Romance* is pronounced with a *th* as in *writhe*, not like the *th* in Smith. See: **lithe**

Boise (Idaho) BOY-see
Also: BOY-zee

boisterous BOY-strus
Don't say: BOY-stir-us

I had an uncle
Who was boisterous
Especially after eating
Half-a-dozen oy-strus

First man: I prefer BOY struss
Second man: I like BOY stir uss
Third man: How about a little peace and quiet?

bologna, buh-LOH-nee (for either spelling)
baloney The Italian city, Bologna, is buh-LOH-ny'h

Two flies found some bologna clinging to the handle of a butcher knife. After eating all they could hold, they took off, only to fall to the ground with a thud. The moral of the story is... don't fly off the handle when you're full of bologna!

bon mot   bohn-MOH
Not as good: bawn-MOH or bahn MOH
The *t* is silent, even in the plural, *bon mots*
(bohn-MOHZ)

bona fide   BO-nuh fyd (rhymes with *ride*)
Avoid: BO-nuh FIGH-dee (rhymes with *tidy*)
Also avoid the expression *bona fides*
(BO-nuh FIGH-deez).

boudoir   BOO-dwahr or boo-DWAHR

bouquet   boo-KAY or bow-KAY

boutique   boo-TEEK
Don't say: bow-TEEK

bowdlerize   BOWD-luh-ryz (BOWD rhymes with *proud*)
Also: BOHD-luh-ryz (BOHD as in *abode*)
Don't say: BOHL-dur-yz

Definition: to prudishly expurgate a piece of writing. *Bowdlerize* derives from the English editor Thomas Bowdler, who rewrote much of Shakespeare, removing profanity and sexual and vulgar references in order to protect what he considered to be the sensibilities of Victorian audiences.

I've always tried to be tasteful with my humor, but almost any joke risks offending someone. One listener wrote me a very concerned but thoughtful letter when she heard this one back in 1968.

A bum asked a man for a quarter for something to eat. The man offered to buy him a drink, wherein the bum said he didn't indulge. The man then offered to buy him a pack of cigarettes. He declined again, saying he didn't smoke, and that he was hungry and wanted something to eat. Whereupon the man said to the bum, "Well, first

*come on home with me...I want my wife to see
what happens to a fella who neither drinks nor
smokes."*

Call it bowdlerizing if you like, but when I told
this joke again in 2002, I changed "bum" to
"panhandler."

bowie knife   BOO-ee knife or BOW-ee knife
Though named after Col. James Bowie, who died
at the Alamo in 1836, and/or his brother Rezin,
bowie is not capitalized in this term.

brethren   BRETH-rin (TH as in *weather*)
Don't say: BRETH-'r-in. *Brethren* has two
syllables, not three.

The insertion of extra vowels in a word sometimes
comes out of nowhere (see: **athlete, biathlon, calm,
decathlon, film, mayoralty, pentathlon, pronunciation**) and sometimes a letter is transposed or
repeated from another syllable of the word (see:
**asphalt, grievous, heinous, larynx, mischievous,
nuptial, realty, sherbet**). See: **spoonerism**

Brisbane   BRIZ-ben in Brisbane, or commonly around
(Australia)   the world: BRIZ-bayn (bayn rhyming with *lane*)
Don't say: BRIZ-bun

British   Most Americans have always been somewhat
dismissive of British pronunciation, finding the
speech of the English at best amusing and at worst
effeminate and absurd. Among well-educated
Americans, however, there has long been a battle
over the proper standard of English pronunciation.
For more than a century after 1776, Anglophiles
were ascendant, taking the view that the only right
way to speak English was the way of the English
upper classes. The English, of course, shared this
view and to this day have not entirely given up

condescending to American English. When I got into radio in 1936, the battle was still raging, but as the U.S. began to overshadow Great Britain as a world power, the emulation of British pronunciation was beginning to wane. H. L. Mencken wrote in *The American Language:* "There was a time when all American actors of any pretensions employed a dialect that was a heavy imitation of the dialect of the West End actors of London. It was taught in all the American dramatic schools, and at the beginning of the [twentieth] century it was so prevalent on the American stage that a flat *a* had a melodramatic effect almost equal to that of damn. But the rise of the movies broke down this convention." Mencken notes that the "pseudo-English standard" favored by early radio announcers for its "chaste and genteel diction" gave way in the late 1930s to what Frank H. Vizetelly of CBS called "the best traditions of American speech." As W. Cabell Greet, Vizetelly's successor at CBS, wrote in 1939: "Most listeners nowadays will sympathize with an announcer who is in revolt against the pseudo-correctness and the insincere voice of the typical announcers of the 20s, who were encouraged in their fake culture by the [American Academy of Arts and Letters'] medal for good diction."

bronchial BRAHN-kee-'l or BRAHNK-yul
Watch out for: BRAHN-ih-kul

One of my listeners wrote me that when he was an intern at Kings County Hospital in Brooklyn, a common complaint of the patients was "bronicle trouble." Soon this local pronunciation sounded quite correct to him. So he said he understood perfectly when an elderly asthmatic patient said to him, "Doc, I'm worried. I got a chronicle bronicle condition."

brooch   brohch
Don't say: brooch

brouhaha   BROO-hah-HAH
Also: broo-HAH-hah

Bryn Mawr   brin MAHR (MAHR sounds like *mar*)
Don't say: brin MOR (MOR rhymes with *for*)

Buckingham   BUCK-ing-um
Avoid: BUCK-ing ham

While BUCK-ing-um is right for the royal palace in London, here in Hartford BUCK-ing-ham is the common pronunciation for the street of that name.

Times were tough in 1930. At age 19, I went to Los Angeles to look for work. I bought this 1926 Chrysler Roadster in California for $65, cleaned it up and sold it for $100.

Buenos Aires   BWAY-nohs AIR-eez
Or BWAY-nohs IGH-rays (sounds like *EYE-race*) if you want to be close to a Spanish pronunciation.

When Babe Ruth made an appearance at Hartford's Bulkeley Stadium in 1940, I was asked to introduce him to the crowd. I was then the host of WTIC's "Strictly Sports," the evening broadcast in which I greeted listeners, "Howdy, sports fans and everybody, how are ya tonight?" and signed off "Your good friend and mine" for some 30 years beginning in 1938.

Bulkeley   BULK-lee
Don't say: BUHK-lee (as in William F. Buckley)

Connecticut Governor and U.S. Senator Morgan G. Bulkeley was the first president of the National League, and so in effect the commissioner of baseball until the "junior circuit" came along. A Hartford high school (mispronounced even by most of its teachers) and a Connecticut river bridge were named after him. So was Hartford's Bulkeley Stadium, off Franklin Avenue in the South End, and for a time, its Eastern League baseball team, the Senators (also the Laurels, the Bees, and the Chiefs). The stadium had a cinder track around the field's perimeter, and the motorcycle races that brought me to Hartford in 1936 as the PA announcer were held there. The Tuesday night races would draw capacity crowds, about 6,500, but after a few years, racing lost its appeal and then in the '50s baseball left too. The stadium was torn down in 1960.

buoy   BOO-ee or boy
But only *boy* when used as a verb

burglar BURG-lur

Don't say: BUR-gyoo-lur

Uncle Carbon went to the police station and asked, "Could I see the burglar who broke into our house last night?

"Why do you want to see him?" the desk sergeant asked.

"I'd like to ask him how he got in without waking my wife."

business BIZ-nis

Avoid: BIH-zih-nes

You may ask why you should pronounce the middle *o* in **sophomore** if you don't pronounce the *i* in the middle of *business*. Further, you might ask why we even try to justify our recommended pronunciations with logic, reason or common sense. Go ahead ask. And if we ever come up with a good answer, we'll give it to you.

If at first you do succeed...it's probably your father's business.

cabal kuh-BAL (BAL rhymes with *pal*)
Avoid: kuh-BAWL

cache kash (sounds like *cash*)
Don't say: kach (sounds like *catch*)
During a rare outside-of-the-Iron-Curtain tour, a midget acrobat of the Prague Circus decided to defect. He presented himself to the American Embassy in France and asked: "Pardon, but can you cache a small Czech?"

cachet ka-SHAY (ka as in *caffeine* and *cat*)
Don't say: ka-SHET

Cadiz KAY-diz
(Spain) Don't say: kuh-DIZ

Cairo KAY-roh
(Missouri) Not like the capital of Egypt: KIGH-roh

California KAL-ih-**FORN**-yuh
Not: KAL-ih-**FORN**-ee-uh
And KAL-ih-**FORN**-eye-ay only in song
    and legend

calm rhymes with *Mom* and *Tom* (one syllable only)
See: **alms, balk, balm, caulk** and **qualm**

Calvary KAL-vuh-ree
Don't confuse with cavalry (KAV-'l-ree), and vice versa.

Canada geese   Don't call them Canadian geese, whether or not they're from north of the border.

Canadiens   In English, the Montreal Canadiens hockey club should be pronounced the same as if this French word were spelled like the English word *Canadians*. It's not kuh-NAY-dee-ENZ even in French. Don't say it as if it were spelled "Canadiennes." Save that pronunciation for the day they get a women's hockey team in Montreal, if then.

While in California I turned my motorcycle competition skills to advantage as an extra and stunt man, in 1934 in "She Couldn't Take It" starring George Raft and Joan Bennett. I played a motorcycle cop and am shown here, on the far right, with my fellow cyclists. I also doubled for Spencer Tracy in 1932 in "Disorderly Conduct."

Canberra   KAN-brah in Australia, or KAN-bur-uh
(Australia)   elsewhere. Don't say: kan-BAIR-uh

candidate   KAN-dih-dayt
Also: KAN-dih-dit
See: **advocate, delegate**

capricious   kuh-PRISH-us
Don't say: kuh-PREE-shus

caramel   KAR-uh-m'l
Don't say: KAHR-mul

Caribbean KAIR-uh-**BEE**-in
Also: kuh-RIB-ee-in

This is one of those words that many people sometimes pronounce one way and sometimes another. They will mostly say KAIR-uh-**BEE**-in when it stands alone, as in "We're going to the Caribbean," but often kuh-RIB-ee-in when using it as an adjective in front of another word, as in Caribbean Sea or Caribbean vacation.
See: **already, -day**

Carpentier, Georges When the French heavyweight boxing champion came to the U.S. in 1921 to challenge the World Champ, Jack Dempsey, the press, oblivious to French pronunciation, saw the *s* on the end of his first name and dubbed him "Gorgeous Georges." The "Manassa Mauler" kayoed the "Orchid Man" in the fourth round.

casualty KAZH-oo-'l-tee
Easier to say, so perhaps inevitable: KAZH-uhl-tee

catty-cornered A variant of cater-cornered. Even though the derivation and meaning of this word have nothing to do with felines, you can also say kitty-cornered. But, either way, *-cornered* is preferable to *-corner.*

Roy Rogers had just bought himself a brand new pair of snazzy cowboy boots and understandably was very proud of them. Before they were a week old, though, they were inadvertently left out overnight on the veranda of his sprawling ranch house in the California mountains. Wouldn't you know, a pesky mountain lion that had been ravaging area farms and ranches, would come along on a moonless night and tear one of those new boots to shreds? He did exactly that and Roy was fit to be tied. Roy grabbed his Winchester, jumped on Trigger and took off for the mountains in the customary cloud of dust, vowing to bring in the carcass of that feline marauder. To make a long story short, he succeeded. Hours later, when Roy's wife, Dale, saw her hubby riding through the gate with the dead lion slung across Trigger's hindquarters, she called out, "Pardon me, Roy. Is that the cat that chewed your new shoe?"

caulk   kawk (rhymes with *walk* and *hawk*)
The *l* is silent. See: **balk, balm, calm** and **qualm**

catsup   KETCH-up
Don't say: CAT-suhp

Catsup, a variant spelling, is pronounced the same as *ketchup*.

cause célèbre   KAWZ say-LEB or KAWZ say-LEB-ruh
Célèbre can also be pronounced like celebrity up to the *b* (celeb). If you want to sound the *re* ending, better to use a word or expression in English. Definition: a celebrated legal case or controversy.

caveat   kay-vee-AT, KA-vee-at or **KAH**-vee-AHT
Definition: a warning

celebratory   SEL-uh-bruh-tor-ee or suh-LEB-ruh-tor-ee

celestial suh-LES-ch'l
Don't say: suh-LES-tee-'l
See: **controversial**

I always felt sorry for Dr. Watson whenever Sherlock Holmes would ridicule him. Once the two were on a camping trip when Holmes woke his associate in the middle of the night and said, "Watson, look up and tell me what you deduce."

Watson looked up, contemplated the stars in the vast heavens above him and finally answered, "I see so many stars that I have to conclude that some of them have planets like ours and that among those planets, it is possible that life could exist."

"Watson, you idiot," said Holmes, "somebody stole our tent!"

Celtic SEL-tik or KEL-tik
The pronunciation of Celtic has a long and complicated history. When it's not spelled Keltic, either pronunciation is correct, although you will hear KEL-tik more often when the subject is history or anthropology.

centenary SEN-tuh-NAIR-ee or sen-TEN-'r-ee

cerebral SAIR-uh-br'l or suh-REE-br'l

chaise longue shayz LAWNG (rhymes with *stays long*)
Don't say: chays LOWNJ (like *chase lounge*)

Don't be fooled just because a chaise longue is a good place to lounge. The expression in French means long chair.

chameleon kuh-MEEL-yuhn or kuh-MEE-lee-'n
Don't say: shuh-MEEL-yuhn

chamois SHAM-ee
Don't say: sham-WAH

chamomile   KAM-uh-myl (myl sounds like *mile*) or
KAM-uh-meel

chasm   kazm
Not: chasm

chassis   CHAS-ee, also SHAS-ee
Don't say: CHAS-is

chauffeur   shoh-FUR or SHOH-f'r
See: **connoisseur, entrepreneur** and other words
from the French ending in *eur*: **amateur, saboteur,
auteur, raconteur, provocateur, restaurateur,
hauteur, liqueur, de rigeur**

*My Uncle Imported is a chauffeur for Mr. and
Mrs. Walker Goode. He delivers the Goodes.*

chic   sheek
Don't say: chik

*"Oh, what a funny looking cow," the chic young
thing from Greenwich said to the farmer. "But
why hasn't it any horns?"*

    *"There are many reasons," the farmer replied,
"why a cow does not have horns. Some do not
have them until late in life. Others are dehorned,
while still other breeds are not supposed to have
horns. This cow does not have horns because it is
a horse."*

Chicago   shih-KAH-goh
Don't say: chih-KAH-goh

*My Uncle Corrugated had one of the biggest
toupee factories in Chicago. Made nothing but
sizes 8½ and 8¾. He had a bright idea and called
in all his toupees from all over the country so he
could make them up in more popular sizes. Made
a big news story. You may remember the head-
lines: "Big wigs called to Chicago."*

chicanery shih-KAY-n'r-ee
Don't say: chih-KAY-n'r-ee

chimerical ky-MEER-uh-k'l or kih-MEER-uh-k'l
Don't say: chih-MEER-uh-k'l or shih-MEER-uh-k'l
Definition: imaginary, unreal, fantastic or
impossible

A 10 TO 1
FAVORITE !

RLS

chinch bug CHINCH bug
Definition: any bug that figures to win easily

Chinese chigh-NEES or chigh-NEEZ
See: **Japanese** and **Portuguese**

chiropodist ky-RAH-puh-dist
Don't say: shir-AHP-uh-dist

chrysanthemum krih-**SAN**-thuh-MUM
Don't say: krih-SAN-thee-UM

civilization SIV-ih-lih-**ZAY**-shin
British: SIV-ih-ligh-**ZAY**-shin

clandestine klan-DES-tin
Not: KLAN-dih-stin or KLAN-dih-steen or
KLAN-dih-styn (rhyming with *wine*) or
KLAN-dih-**STYN**
Nor: klan-DES-teen or klan-DES-tyn

clique kleek
Don't say: klik

clothier KLOTH-yur or KLO-thee-ur
Don't say: klo-thee-AY
See: **hotelier**

coercion koh-UR-shun
Don't say: koh-UR-zhun

English has lots of words ending in *sion* (zhun),
many ending in *tion* (shun), quite a few ending in
ssion (shun) and some ending in *cian* (shin), but
cion (shun) is a rarity. *Coercion* should no more
be said with a *zh* than *suspicion or physician* or
musician, mission or *commission*, or *assertion,
desertion, exertion, insertion, addition, ambition*
or *tradition*. Just as you wouldn't substitue an
sh sound for a *zh* in words like *division, decision,
collision, provision* or *precision*, don't give
coercion a *zh* sound.

cognoscenti KAHG-nuh-**SEN**-tee or KAHN-yuh-shen-tee
Avoid: KOH-nyoh-**SHEN**-tee

*Cognoscent*i is an Italian plural meaning experts,
especially in the fine arts. The singular is
cognoscente (KAHG-nuh-**SEN**-tay).

Coleridge KOHL-rij
(Samuel Taylor) Don't say: KOH-ler-ij

collate kahl-LAYT (LAYT sounds like *late*), kahl-AYT
or KOH-layt. Although collate has two *l*'s, one in
each syllable, one or the other is often ignored.

collectible Be careful not to spell this word with an *a* instead
of an *i*. We know of no rules to help determine
which words end in *able* (*capable, movable,*

durable, reliable, adorable, etc.) and which end in *ible* (*possible, reversible, sensible, compatible, convertible*, etc.) and getting them right is sometimes a challenge.

Speaking of spelling, for some reason, to judge from my mail, a great many WTIC listeners seem to think my first name has two o's.

collegiality kuh-LEE-jee-**AL**-ih-tee
Avoid: kuh-LEE-gee-**AL**-ih-tee

Colleague may seem closer to *collegiality*, but think of *college* or *collegian*. *Collegiality* and *colleague* both derive from the same Latin root as *college*; *collegiality* doesn't come from *colleague*.

colloquial kuh-LOH-kwee-'l
Don't say: kuh-LOH-kee-'l

column KAHL-'m
Don't say: KAHL-yoom or KAHL-yum

combatant kum-BAT-n't
Also: KAHM-buh-t'nt

To protect yourself from muggers, go to a Kung Fu school... and stay there.

comity KAHM-ih-tee
Don't say: KOH-mih-tee
Definition: mutual courtesy, civility

commingle kuh-MING-'l or kum-MING-'l
Don't say: KOH-ming-'l or koh-MING-'l

Note the two *m*'s. This word begins with *com*, not *co*.

commitment Although *committed* and *committal* have the double *t*, *commitment* has one. Generally, a *t* is doubled before a vowel, not a consonant.

comparable KAHM-p'r-uh-b'l
Don't say: kum-PAIR-uh-b'l

It seems odd that some of the same people who don't want to put the stress on the first syllable in *comparable* and say kum-PAIR-uh-b'l will nonetheless say KAHN-suh-mit for *consummate*, getting both adjectives wrong. Proper pronunciation is not always logical, but those who follow their own rules in mispronouncing words might at least show a little consistency.

In 1934 I began doing public address system announcing of motorcycle races in California. This photo was taken on Wilshire Boulevard in L.A.

comptroller kun-TROH-lur (just like *controller*—which is the same thing)
Avoid: KAHMP-troh-lur

A comptroller is a controller. *Comptroller* was likely brought into the language and retained as a fancy way to spell *controller*.

conch kahnch or kahngk (sounds like *conk*)

Concord, concord The town in Massachusetts where the shot heard round the world was fired in 1775 is KAHNGK-'rd (sounds like *conquered*). Same for the capital of New Hampshire, and the grape and its wine are pronounced the same way. But most other towns of the same name in the U.S., the name of the Anglo-French supersonic airliner, and the word for agreement or harmony are pronounced KAHN-kord or KAHNG-kord

conflagration KAHN-fluh-**GRAY**-sh'n
Don't say: kuhn-**FLAG**-uh-RAY-sh'n

connoisseur kahn-uh-SUR (uh-SUR rhymes with *officer*)
Don't say: kahn-uh-SOOR

There's no s*ewer* in *connoisseur*.

Words from the French ending in *eur* should be consistently pronounced as if they were spelled without the *u*. In fact, I wish we would spell them without the *u*. The *eur* should rhyme with *sir* and *fighter*. Hardly anyone has a problem with *chauffeur* or *voyeur*. You never hear shoh-FOOR or shoh-FYOOR, voy-OOR or voy-YOOR. And most get *amateur* correct. Even in *pasteurization*, you hear PAS-chur-ih-**ZAY**-sh'n as well as PAS-tur-ih-**ZAY**-sh'n, but never PAS-choor-ih-**ZAY**-sh'n. Yet when it comes to *connoisseur*, too many try to get fancy, leading them into the *sewer*!

See **entrepreneur** and other words from the French ending in *eur*: **amateur, saboteur, auteur, raconteur, chauffeur, provocateur, restaurateur, hauteur, liqueur, de rigeur, voyeur,** (Guy) **LeFleur**

consortium kun-SOR-she-um
Avoid: kun-SORT-ee-um or kun-SOR-shum or kun-SOR-see-um

consul, KAHN-s'l, KAHN-suh-lit
consulate Don't say: KOWN-s'l, KOWN-suh-lit

consummate kun-SUM-it
(adj.) Don't say: KAHN-suh-mit

I know what you're thinking. Why are you advised to accent the first syllable in *consulate* but not in *consummate* (as an adjective)? Is it any wonder people start putting the stress on the first syllable in *consummate* as well? Despite the gradual tendency in English to move stress toward the first syllable, *consummate* as an adjective is still kun-SUM-it.

contractual   kuhn-TRAK-tyoo-'l
Don't say: kuhn-TRAK-tyur-'l
There's no *r* near the end of *contractual.*

contrasting   kuhn-TRAST-een
Don't say: KAHN-trast-een
See: **baptise, default, increase**

controversial   KAHN-truh-**VER**-sh'l
Just as you wouldn't say Californ-i-a,
Don't say: KAHN-truh-**VER**-she-'l or
KAHN-truh-**VER**-see-'l.

There's something a little prissy about KAHN-truh-**VER**-see-'l, even worse than pronouncing *negotiate* nuh-GO-see-ayt. The fact that the *ia* combination in *negotiate* and *associate*, as well as in *poinsettia*, is pronounced as two syllables, not one, may be what makes some think the *ia* in *controversial* should be pronounced as two syllables. Think instead of the *ia* in *paraphernalia, penitentiary* and *beneficial.* You wouldn't say BEN-uh-**FIH**-see-'l. *Beneficial* ends in the same *sh'l* sound as *controversial.* Also think of the many words that end in *tial,* such as *spatial, partial, martial, initial, essential, potential, tangential, deferential, influential, confidential, substantial,* **bestial, celestial** and **nuptial.**

Copenhagen   **KOH**-p'n-HAY-g'n
Avoid: **KOH**-p'n-HAH-g'n

corpus delicti Why do we sometimes hear *corpus delecti* instead of the correct *corpus delicti*? Being murdered is offense enough. One's corpse shouldn't have to suffer a further indignity. Especially when *delecti* suggests delectable, not at all what *delicti* means, coming from the Latin *delinquere*–to do something wrong. The corpus delicti is the body of the murder victim, a legal term. The reason for the mispronunciation no doubt is due to confusion with *delectable*. Think instead of *derelict*. And look at that *i* in the middle. This point is one detectives from C. Auguste Dupin (aw-GOOST doo-PAN) to Sherlock Holmes would no doubt appreciate. We do not see what is right under our noses. In the same way, many look at **etc.** and think *ect.*, pronouncing it *ek cetera*. Or the *h* in **asphalt** is misplaced and out comes *ashphalt*. Or the *i* in **heinous, grievous** or **mischievous** is moved in front of the last syllable so that we hear *henious, grevious* and *mischevious*.

corsage kor-SAHZH
Don't say: kor-SAHJ
See: **garage**

Cosby (Bill) KAHZ-bee
Avoid: KAWZ-bee

Costa Rica KOH-stuh REE-kuh
Avoid: KAH-stuh REE-kuh

costume KAHS-toom
Don't say: KAHS-tyoom

coup de grâce koo d' GRAHS (GRAHS rhymes with first syllable of *pasta*)
Don't say: koo d' GRAH

Grâce is one of those words that are often mispronounced by people who should know better–

and so sound especially bad. Of course a great many people who don't make words their business mispronounce words and nobody ever pays any attention. But educated people, the kind of people likely to use a phrase like coup de grâce, as well as people in the radio and television business, shouldn't make this mistake. No doubt, they're just not paying attention. If one part of the brain tells them, correctly that *grâce*, just like *grace*, has an *s* sound, another, half-educated part of the brain tells them that *s* at the end of French words is usually silent (thinking of, say, pâtè de foie gras), so they stumble into saying koo d' GRAH, no doubt complimenting themselves on their polish. A similar mental error may explain the mispronunciation of *vichyssoise*.

coupon	KOO-pahn Also: KYOO-pahn
Coventry (Connecticut)	KAH-v'n-tree In England, it's KUH-v'n-tree
covert	KOH-vurt or KUH-vert Don't be misled by *overt* into saying koh-VURT
coyote	ky-YOH-tee, ky-OH-tee or KY-oht You can run free with this word.
crevasse	kruh-VAS Don't say: KREH-vus. A crevasse is a deep crevice, especially in a glacier, and is sometimes confused with and pronounced like *crevice*.
crèche	kresh Avoid: kraysh and krech

crescendo   kruh-SHEN-doh
Don't say: kruh-SEN-doh

crisis, crises   KRY-sis, KRY-seez

Cristobal   krih-STOH-b'l
(Panama)   Don't say: krih-stoh-BAHL

croissant   kwah-SOHNT or kwah-SAHNT

cul de sac   KUL d' sak
Avoid: KYOOL d' sak

culinary   **KYOO**-lih-NAIR-ee or **KUHL**-ih-NAIR-ee

cupola   KYOO-puh-luh
Don't say: KOO-puh-luh

When in doubt about how to pronounce the *u* in a word, *oo* is your best bet, but there are many exceptions. Besides **cupola**, for example, there's **culinary, curator** and **ubiquitous.**

curator   KYOOR-ay-t'r or kyuh-RAY-t'r

cycle, cyclic, cyclical   The long *i* is preferable, but a short *i* is acceptable, especially in *cyclical*, which is a little easier to say with a short *i*.

cynosure   Again, the *i* sound can go either way.
Definition: a center of attraction

dachshund   DAHKS-hoond or DAHKS-hoont
Don't say: DASH-hound

A listener from Vernon wrote, "I call my Dachshund 'Pumpernickel' because she's German bred." And a kennel owner in Litchfield advertised dachshund puppies for sale with the sign ... "git a *long* little doggie."

daguerreotype   duh-GAIR-oh-typ (typ sounds like *type*)
Don't say: duh-GAIR-ee-oh-typ

The word comes from photography pioneer, Louis Daguerre (duh-GAIR), so don't twist the *guerre* into two syllables.

daiquiri   DY-kuh-ree
Don't say: DAK-uh-ree

There was a doctor who arrived at his favorite bar at the same time each evening and ordered a chestnut daiquiri. So the bartender would make his drink just before he arrived. One night, as the bartender began to mix the chestnut daiquiri, he discovered he was out of chestnuts. Worried, he searched high and low. Finally he found an old, wizened hickory nut. Thinking quickly, the bartender ground up the hickory nut and sprinkled it over the daiquiri. The doctor arrived, took one sip of his drink, looked at the bartender, and said, "This isn't a chestnut daiquiri." "No," the bartender answered. "It's a hickory daiquiri, Doc!"

dais DAY-is

Don't say: DY-is

Suddenly coming upon words not often used can be a shock. It's hard to think quickly of how to say *dais*. In fact, Alfred Hitchcock once considered doing a movie about a speaker into whose text this inconspicuous murderer of oratorical reputations had been secretly inserted. It is a little humiliating to get a four-letter word wrong. Perhaps that's why some dictionaries have given in and cite a common mistake as an acceptable pronunciation: DIGH-iss. Keeping some logic in the language is a worthy goal. The letter combination *ai* is usually sounded *ay*, as in *rain*, and sometimes *eh*, as in *said*, but even if you pronounce it *eye* in *dais*, wouldn't you end up with *dice*? (Amazingly, *dice* is sometimes given as well.) Where would you get another *i* in order to come up with DIGH-iss?

Recipe for a good speech: Add shortening!

Sirs:
I made this drawing all by myself. And I'm only 33 years old.
Bob Steele
Hartford, Conn.

From Life magazine, Letters to the Editor, January 22, 1945

DALI WITH A HOLE
IN HIS STOCKIN'

Dalí dah-LEE (for *Dalí* with the accented *ì*)
(Salvador) Also: DAHL-ee (sounds like *Dolly*) when spelled *Dali* (unaccented *i*)

The Americanization of the pronunciation of this artist's name was no doubt furthered by the lack of accent marks on typewriters. The change has been both in pronunciation and spelling. Many dictionaries give only Americanized pronunciation, and some give only the anglicized spelling. Indeed, *Dali* (unaccented) is probably found more often in print than *Dalì* (accented). The dropping of accent marks seems to be an inevitable result of fame in this country, but we wonder if this kind of Americanization of so much of our world is always a good thing. The flamboyant twentieth century Spanish artist did spend time in the U.S., including in Hartford, thanks to legendary Wadsworth Atheneum director Chick Austin, but he probably would no more have given up his accented ì than his famous mustache. See **Martì**.

Darien dair-ee-EN
(Connecticut) Don't say: DAIR-ee-en

data DAYT-uh or DAT-uh (DAT-uh rhymes with *at a*)
See: **status**

day -day or -dee in the days of the week. And whether you say, for example, Sun*day* or Sun*dee* in a given situation may depend on the rhythm, accent and syntax of your speech. You don't have to be consistent. A similar slurring leads many to turn *t* into *d* in words like *ninety*, or, worse, *d* into *t*, yielding *hundret* for *hundred*.

daylight saving Saving, not savings. Say "daylight *saving* time," not "daylight *savings* time," unless, perhaps, if you're on the way to make several bank deposits or purchases at a discount store.

de rigeur DEE rih-**GUR** (GUR as in *finger*).
Don't say: DEE rih-**GYOOR** or day ree-GAIR
See: **connoisseur, entrepreneur** and other words
from the French ending in *eur*: **amateur, saboteur,
auteur, raconteur, chauffeur, provocateur,
restaurateur, hauteur, liqueur, voyeur**

decal d'-KAL
Also: DEE-kal

decathlon d'-KATH-lahn
Don't say: d'KATH-uh-lahn
See: **pentathlon, triathlon** and **biathlon**
*I had a friend who was a great athlete. He wasn't
too smart, a little slow on the draw, but he won a
gold medal in the Olympics. He was so excited he
said he was going to have it bronzed.*

default d'-FAWLT
Unless you're a lawyer, never say DEE-fawlt,
either as a noun or a verb. Many two-syllable
verbs shift pronunciation from back to front
when used as nouns (e.g. *addict, combat,
decrease, increase, insult, protest*). *Default* is not
among them.

defendant d'-FEN-d'nt or dee-FEN-d'nt, d'-FEND-'nt
or dee-FEND-'nt
Avoid: d'-FEN-dant

The strange and cacophonous habit of many
lawyers in pronouncing this word d'-FEN-dant,
and even d'-fen-DANT, is negligent, if not criminal. The error may derive from confusion with
legal terms which are distinguished from each
other by their suffixes, and which accordingly get
the emphasis–words such as *lessor* and *lessee,
mortgagor* and *mortgagee, assignor* and *assignee.*
Shakespeare's King Richard II refers to "the accus-
er and the accused," giving *accused* three syllables,

but only to fit the iambic meter of the line. The error even carries over to infect the pronunciation of *appellant* as uh-pel-ANT instead of the correct uh-PEL-'nt. The mispronunciation uh-pel-ANT seemingly emphasizes that the party is not an appellee. But it is hardly necessary to call a party a d'-fen-DANT to distinguish him or her from a plaintiff or a prosecutor.

Defense and *offense* are usually stressed on the second syllable, but when they refer to an attack or to a side or a team, in order to emphasize their polar quality, the stress in each shifts to the first syllable.

deity DEE-ih-tee
Avoid: DAY-ih-tee
See: **heterogeneity, homogeneity, simultaneity, spontaneity**

delinquent dih-LING-kwent
Don't say: dih-LIN-kwent

True, there's no *g* in *delinquent*, but there is an *ng* sound in its pronunciation. See: **relinquish**.

Uncle Tempered hates to be disturbed when he's watching his favorite TV program, and is particularly aroused when his neighbors' unruly kids start dashing around his backyard. The other evening they went galloping through his garage. "Do that again," he yelled after them, "and I'll call the police!" One of the kids yelled back, "Who do you think is after us now?"

deluge DEL-yooj
Don't say: d'-LOOJ

demur d'-MUR (MUR rhymes with *fur*)
Don't say: d'-MYOOR
Definition: to object

demure d'-MYOOR
Don't say: d'MUR
Definition: modest, shy

denigrate DEH-nih-grayt
A listener wrote me once that this word is not always used in a derogatory context, as when the boss says, "You've denigrate job!"

Des Moines d' MOYN
(Iowa) Don't say: d' MOYNZ

despicable d'-SPIK-uh-b'l or DES-pik-uh-b'l

desultory **DES**-uhl-TOR-ee
Don't say: **DEZ**-uhl-TOR-ee

deteriorate dih-TEER-ee-uh-rayt
Watch out for: dih-TEER-uh-rayt. Pronounce all five syllables.

Detroit dih-TROIT
Don't say: DEE-troit

Devilish Dozen *Master even just these 12 most common mispronunciations and you'll be way ahead of a lot of otherwise well-educated people.*

alleged uh-LEJD (rhymes with *edged*); not: uh-LEJ-id
connoisseur kahn-uh-SUR (rhymes with *officer*); not: kahn-uh-SOOR
coup de grâce koo d' GRAHS; not: koo d' GRAH
entrepreneur AHN-truh-pruh-**NUR** (rhymes with *fur*); not: AHN-truh-pruh-**NOOR**
espresso eh-SPRES-oh or es-PRES-oh; not: ek-SPRES-oh
et cetera et SET-'r-uh; not: ek-SET-'r-uh or ek-SEH-truh
integral IN-tuh-grul; not: in-TEG-rul or IN-truh-gul;

lackadaisical	LACK-uh-**DAY**-zih-k'l; not: LAX-uh-**DAY**-zih-k'l
mischievous	MIS-chih-vus; not: mis-CHEE-vee-us
nuclear	NOO-klee-ur; not: NOO-kyuh-lur or NOO-kyoo-lur
nuptial	NUHP-sh'l (tial as in *partial*); not: NUHP-shoo-'l or NUP-choo-'l
succinct	suhk-SINGKT; not: suh-SINGKT

---

diaper DY-pur or DY-uh-pur
The safety pin is now 120 years old, but there have been a lot of changes since it was invented.

diaspora dy-AS-pur-uh
Don't say: DY-uh-SPOR-uh
Definition: the migration of people who have a common origin or common beliefs

didactic digh-DAK-tik
Cousin Thespian Steele was a Broadway star. He became deathly ill one night, but he refused to skip the performance and he DIDACTIC!

diesel DEE-z'l
Don't say: DEE-s'l

different than   *Imply* is a more common word <u>than</u> *infer* but it's not different <u>than</u> *infer*; it's different <u>from</u> *infer*.

dilapidated   dih-LAP-ih-**DAY**-t'd
Don't say: dih-LAP-ih-**TAY**-t'd

With "Joltin' Joe" DiMaggio at Yankee spring training camp in Fort Lauderdale. A few years earlier I was at Yankee Stadium to present Joe with a new Cadillac, a gift from his fans in Hartford. It was just what he needed. I met him at his hotel in New York and we drove to the Bronx in his car, an old, beat-up Caddy. Yanks lost to the Red Sox that day, 3-0 in 11 innings.

DiMaggio   dih-MAH-jee-oh (MAH as in *Ma* and *Pa*)
Don't say: dih-MAH-zhee-oh or dih-MA-zhee-oh (MA as in *mat*)

And don't forget to capitalize the M.

I once asked Red Sox centerfielder Dom DiMaggio, "Who's the best hitter, your teammate Ted Williams or your brother Joe DiMaggio of the Yankees?"

After pausing just for a moment, Dom replied, "Ted's the best left-handed hitter in baseball today and my brother Joe the best right-handed batter."

diminution   DIM-ih-**NOO**-shun
Watch out for DIM-yoo-**NIH**-shun.

diocese, diocesan   DY-uh-sees (sounds like *cease*) or
DY-uh-sis, dy-AHS-ih-sin

diphtheria dif-THEER-ee-uh
Avoid: dip-THEER-ee-uh
See: **diphthong, naphtha, ophthalmologist**

diphthong DIF-thawng
Avoid: DIP-thawng

dirigible DEER-ih-jih-b'l
Not as good: di-RIJ-ih-b'l

Not Bonnie and Clyde, but Shirley and Bob. Shirley Hanson of West Hartford was working at the Travelers in 1937, in the same building that housed WTIC's studios. I first saw her on the elevator. We were engaged that fall, then eloped and married January 10, 1938 It was her pronunciation of smörgåsbord that swept me off my feet.

dishabille dis-uh-BEEL
Avoid: dis-uh-BIL

Two friends were wending through West Farms Mall when one of them stopped to gaze dazedly at a sign.
  "Whatchu lookin' at? said the other.
  "That sign."
  "Whazzit say?"
  "Ladies' Ready to Wear Clothes."
  "Dern near time, if anyone was to ask me,"
came the reply.

disparate DIS-puh-rit
Don't say: dis-PAIR-it

dissect dih-SEKT
Don't say: DY-sekt or dy-SEKT
Don't be fooled by *bisect* (prefix *bi*). There are two *s*'s in dissect because the prefix is *dis*, not *di*.

disputant dih-SPYOOT-'nt or DIHS-pyoo-t'nt

divan DY-van or dih-VAN

diverse dih-VURS
Also: dy-VURS

divisive d'-VY-siv
Don't say: d'-VIS-iv

When Phil made his announcement as a candidate for Congress in Connecticut's first district in 1992, he did it over the radio. Dad was listening. When I spoke to Phil later, I said, "You sounded great, except for one thing: *d'-VIS-iv.* You mispronounced *divisive.*" Some do say *d'-VIS-iv,* probably taking their cue from *division* rather than *divide.* With that kind of divisive example within a family of words, civil war may be inevitable. Phil, happily for this family, and this book, now goes with *d'-VY-siv.*

docile DAHS-'l
Don't say: DAHS-yl (yl sounds like *aisle*)
See: **fertile, fragile, futile, hostile, mobile, servile, versatile** and **volatile**

They say big, strong men make docile husbands. So do big, strong women.

doggonest, doggonedest, Possibly the only superlative form in English that has no comparative form (*doggoner, doggoneder?*), *doggone [it],* an interjection, a verb, and an adjective, most likely arose as a euphemism for *God damn it,* and is usually defined as damned or confounded, or a synonym for hang or drat, but one dictionary now defines it as an exclamation expressing annoyance, surprise or *pleasure.* Any word that can express either annoyance or pleasure is worthy of special notice. While most dictionaries give both *doggone* and *doggoned,* few even note the superlative form, and none we've found gives *doggonest,* so we'd advise pronouncing, and writing, a second *d* sound: daw-GAWND-'st for what clearly is the *doggonedest* entry in this book. Such a word invites innovation, however, and some apparently favor simplicity, figuring that *gone* shouldn't require a *d,* or [e]*d* in or out of this word. One animal lover has written a series of popular children's books like *The Doggonest Christmas,* and that form of the word may better capture the milder and quirky sense now most often meant.

I arrived in Hartford in May of 1936. Here I'm standing next to the Travelers Insurance Co. in the summer of 1937. Just hours before I was scheduled to leave town to return to California, I landed a job as a staff announcer at WTIC, the 50,000-watt clear channel radio station owned by the Travelers.

domicile DAH-mih-syl (syl rhymes with *file*) or DAH-mih-sil
Avoid: DOH-mih-syl and DOH-mih-sil
See: **docile, fertile, fragile, futile, hostile, mobile, servile, versatile** and **volatile.** While *domicile* can take the American short *i* pronunciation in the last

syllable, like **juvenile** and **textile**, it is more often pronounced in the British manner with a long *i*.

The minister: "Life begins at birth."
The priest: "Life begins at conception."
The rabbi: "You're both wrong. Life begins when the kids all leave home and the dog dies."

double   double ahn-TAHN-druh
entendre   We strongly discourage giving this expression too much of a French pronunciation, turning the *duh* of double into *doo*—no double meaning intended.

dour   DOOR (rhymes with *tour*) or DOWR (rhymes with *hour*)
Also: DUR (rhymes with *fur*)

A man found a lamp, picked it up and rubbed it. Out popped a genie with a dour expression on his face. "Okay," says the genie, "You released me from the lamp. Blah, blah, blah. This is the fourth time this month. You can forget about three. You only get one wish."

The man sat and thought about it for a while and then said, "I've always wanted to go to Hawaii, but I'm scared to fly, and I get very seasick. Could you build me a bridge to Hawaii, so I could drive over there to visit?"

The genie laughed and said, "That's impossible. Just think of the logistics. Think of how far the supports would have to reach to the bottom of the Pacific! Think of how much concrete, how much steel–no, think of another wish."

The guy said okay and tried to think of another wish. Finally he said, "I've been married and divorced four times. My wives always said that I don't care and that I'm insensitive, so I wish that I could understand women, know how they feel inside and what they're thinking when they give me the silent treatment, know why they're crying, know what they really want when they say nothing, know how to make them truly happy."

The genie looked at the man for a moment and then said, "You want that bridge two lanes or four?"

drowned drownd
Don't say: DROWN-ded

Drown doesn't end in *d*. The past tense adds e*d* but not a syllable, just a *d* sound. It's not like *pound* which becomes *pounded*.

DuBois doo-BOYS (BOYS rhymes with *Royce* and *voice*.)
(W.E.B.) Don't say: DOO-boys or doo-BWAH

W.E.B. DuBois (1868-1941) was an American writer, poltical thinker and founder of the NAACP who advocated civil rights and black nationalism.

duces tecum DOO-chis TAY-kum
Common among lawyers: DOOk-kis TEE-kum

A subpoena duces tecum requires the party served to produce documents in his or her possession.

July, 1946. Dad gives Robert, age 7, a lesson in the art of pugilism.

Dwayne, Dwight dwayn, dwyt
Don't say: duh-WAYN, duh-WYT
Tighten it up. You wouldn't say here's the house where I *duh-well*.

ebullient ih-BUL-yint (BUL rhymes with *lull*)
Avoid: ee-BOO-lee-int or ee-BYOO-lee-int

economic EK-uh-**NAH**-mik or EE-kuh-**NAH**-mik
Of course, money isn't everything, but it helps you keep in touch with the children.

Edinburgh ED-'n-bur-uh
Don't say: ED-'n-burg (except in Edinburgh, Texas)

The Scottish accent bends quite a few pronunciations we would consider standard. For example, *louse* sounds like *loose*.

A Scot who paid a visit to Canada had never seen a moose. When he saw one for the first time, he asked what it was.

"That's a moose," said his host.

"If that's a MOOSE," the Scot replied, "how big are the RATS around here?"

education EJ-yoo-**KAY**-sh'n or EJ-ih-**KAY**-sh'n
See: **arduous**

A bright young University of Connecticut student thought he could talk his way out of anything. Stumped by a tough mid-year exam, he wrote this excuse across the cover: "Only God knows the answer. Merry Christmas!"

He got the test back, marked: "God gets an A. You get an F."

egregious ih-GREE-jus
Don't say: ih-GREE-jee-us

The *i* turns the second *g* into a *j* (a tie bar), so there's no *i* left to be a separate vowel. See **arduous**

either I once asked Prof. Macintosh of Yale to straighten me out on the word *either*. I asked, "Is it *EE-thur* or *EYE-thur*?" Without hesitation, he replied, "*AY-thur* one, lad, is cor-r-rect!"

electoral ih-LEK-t′r-′l
Don't say: ih-lek-TOR-′l; that would be like saying ih-lek-TRIK-′l for electrical.
See: **mayoral**

eleemosynary EL-uh-**MAHS**-ih-nair-ee
Definition: charitable or relating to charity

elegiac EL-ih-**JY**-ik (JY rhymes with *my*)
Don't say: EL-ih-**JAY**-ik

elementary EL-uh-**MEN**-t′-ree
Be careful of: EL-uh-**MEN**-tree

elm *Elm* has one syllable. Don't say EL-um tree. A similar mistake some make is to turn *film* into two syllables. See: **alms, balk, balm, qualm**

Elysian ih-LIZH-'n
Don't say: ee-LEES-ee-'n
Definition: happy, delightful.

enclave EN-klayv
Don't say: AHN-klayv

England ING-gluhnd (ING rhymes with *sting*)
Don't say: ING-land or ENG-gluhnd

English Among the many pronunciation challenges of English are words that have identical spelling but different pronunciations:

She did not *object* to the *object*. We had to *subject* the *subject* to questioning. A farm can *produce* produce. The *present* is a good time to *present* the *present*. The bandage was *wound* around the *wound*. He spent last *evening evening* out a pile of dirt. The dump was so full it had to *refuse refuse*. The *dove dove* into the bushes. The insurance for the *invalid* was *invalid*. They were too *close* to the door to *close* it. After a *number* of injections of novacaine, his jaw got *number*. We need to *polish* the *Polish* furniture. He could *lead* if he could get the *lead* out. The soldier decided to *desert* in the *desert*. She was kind enough to *present* the *present*. In his *bass* voice he ordered the sea *bass*. They had a *row* about who was to *row*. The buck *does* funny things when the *does* are around. A seamstress and a *sewer* fell into the *sewer*. The farmer taught his *sow* to *sow*. The *wind* was too strong to *wind* the sail. Seeing the *tear* in the painting, he shed a *tear*.

enlightening en-LIGHT-'n-een
Don't say: en-LIGHT-neen
It's okay to shorten the next-to-last syllable, but don't leave it out entirely.

en masse en MASS or ohn MAHS
When you can, try to avoid pronunciations in between English and French, such as ahn MAHS or en MAHS. See: **French**

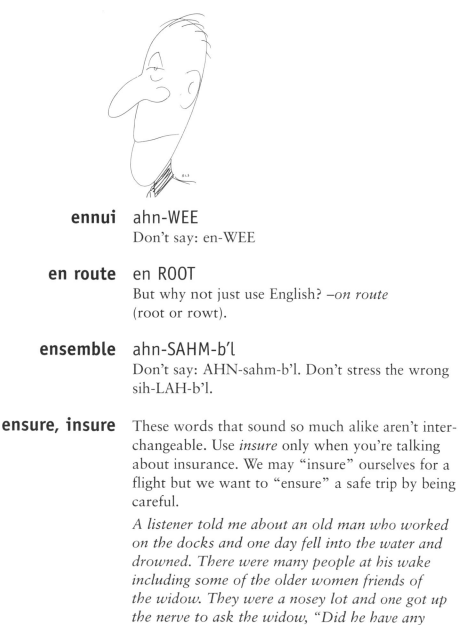

ennui ahn-WEE
Don't say: en-WEE

en route en ROOT
But why not just use English? *—on route* (root or rowt).

ensemble ahn-SAHM-b'l
Don't say: AHN-sahm-b'l. Don't stress the wrong sih-LAH-b'l.

ensure, insure These words that sound so much alike aren't inter-changeable. Use *insure* only when you're talking about insurance. We may "insure" ourselves for a flight but we want to "ensure" a safe trip by being careful.

A listener told me about an old man who worked on the docks and one day fell into the water and drowned. There were many people at his wake including some of the older women friends of the widow. They were a nosey lot and one got up the nerve to ask the widow, "Did he have any insurance?"

The widow answered, "Yes, a fifty thousand dollar policy."

One of her friends turned to another and said, "And him that couldn't read nor write."

The widow stuck her nose in and said, "Nor swim."

entrée AHN-tray or ahn-TRAY

entrepreneur AHN-truh-pruh-**NUR**
Don't say: AHN-truh-pruh-**NOOR** or AHN-truh-pruh-**NYOOR**
See: **connoisseur** and other words from the French ending in *eur*: **amateur, saboteur, auteur, raconteur, chauffeur, provocateur, restaurateur, hauteur, liqueur, de rigeur, voyeur**

Some day a smart fella will come along and get us to spell this word *entreprener*–dropping the *u* just as we dropped the *u* in British spellings such as *favour, colour* and *neighbour.*

There have been many attempts to reform the spelling of English. Our favorite was Mark Twain's "Plan for the Improvement of English Spelling":

For example, in Year 1 that useless letter "c" would be dropped to be replased either by "k" or "s", and likewise "x" would no longer be part of the alphabet. The only kase in which "c" would be retained would be the "ch" formation, which will be dealt with later. Year 2 might reform "w" spelling, so that "which" and "one" would take the same konsonant, wile Year 3 might well abolish "y" replasing it with "i" and Iear 4 might fiks the "g/j" anomali wonse and for all.

Jenerally, then, the improvement would kontinue iear bai iear with Iear 5 doing awai with useless double konsonants, and Iears 6-12 or so modifaiing vowlz and the rimeining voist and unvoist konsonants. Bai Iear 15 or sou, it wud fainali bi posibl tu meik ius ov thi ridandant letez "c", "y" and "x" — bai now jast a memori in the maindz ov ould doderez — tu riplais "ch", "sh", and "th" rispektivli.

Fainali, xen, aafte sam 20 iers ov orxogrefkl riform, wi wud hev a lojikl, kohirnt speling in ius xrewawt xe Ingliy-spiking werld.

envelope EN-vuh-lohp or AHN-vuh-lohp

envoy EN-voy or AHN-voy

epicurean EHP-ih-kyoo-**REE**-in
Also: EHP-ih-**KYUR**-ee-in

Here I capture my favorite subject on camera, March, 1947.

epitome ih-PIT-uh-mee
Don't say: EP-ih-tohm

equanimity EE-kwuh-**NIM**-ih-tee or EK-wuh-**NIM**-ih-tee

equinox EE-kwih-nahks
Don't say: EH-kwih-nahks

Eros EHR-ahs (EHR as in *air*, ahs as in *MS-DOS* and golfer *Jay Haas*) or EER-ahs
Avoid: EHR-ohs
See: **pathos, bathos, ethos** and **kudos**

err ur (rhymes with *her*)
Also: air

Words like *error, erroneous* and *errant*, not to mention *berry, ferry merry, sherry, Perry* and *Terry*, lead many to pronounce *err air*, but in radio broadcasting, *air* is an important verb as well as noun. We air programs. We air commercials. We put them on the air. But when we goof, we *ur*, we don't *air*.

My boss used to say:
To err is human, to forgive, divine
But get it right, you little swine!

escalate, escalator ES-kuh-LAYT, ES-kuh-LAYT-ur
Watch out for: ES-kyoo-LAYT

The culprit behind the improper ES-kyoo-LAYT may be the word *osculate*. Just remember, a kiss is still a kiss but *osculate* has never been *escalate*.

The Shakespeare of West Simsbury, Randy Christensen, once sent me this stock market report: "Helium was up, feathers were down, paper was stationary, knives were up sharply, hiking equipment was trailing, elevators rose while escalators continued their slow decline, weights were up in heavy trading, light switches were off, mining equipment hit rock bottom, diapers remained unchanged." When it comes to stocks, I like to look long range, so I own General Telescope.

escape e-SKAYP
Never say: ek-SKAYP
There's no *x* in *escape*.

eschew es-CHOO
Don't say: eh-SHOO or eh-SKYOO

espionage ES-pee-uh-nahzh
Don't say: ES-pee-uh-nahj
See: **garage, corsage, sabotage**

espresso eh-SPRES-oh or es-PRES-oh
Never: eks-PRES-oh (unless you're in a big hurry!)

Esquire ES-kwyr or es-KWYR (kwyr sounds like *choir*)
Though traditionally a term of courtesy reserved for men and commonly used for attorneys, Esquire (or Esq.) is now used for women as well, especially female attorneys. Now that male attorneys no longer have its exclusive use, however, they seem to use it less.

et al. et AL
Don't say: et AWL

et cetera et SET-'r-uh
Don't say: ek-SET-'r-uh or ek-SEH-truh

ethos EE-thahs (rhymes with *MS-DOS* and *Haas*, as in golfer Jay Haas)
Don't say: EE-thaws or EE-thohs
See: **pathos, bathos, Eros** and **kudos**

eucalyptus Eucalyptus is not too hard to pronounce but it's not easy to spell, at least not for everybody.

Emily Sue passed away and Bubba called 911. The operator told Bubba that she would send someone out right away. "Where do you live?" she asked.

Bubba replied, "At the end of Eucalyptus Drive."

The operator asked, "Can you spell that for me?"

There was a long pause and finally Bubba said, "How about if I drag her over to Oak Street and you pick her up there?"

Uncle STAINLESS bought himself a double decker bus so he can go to drive-in movies. He likes to sit in the balcony.

evening EEV-ning

Don't say: EEV-en-ing, unless you're talking about getting even.

The problem some have with this word may be trying too hard to be correct. Don't be misled by *even* in *evening*. It's pronounced with two syllables, not three.

Evers EE-v'rs
(Johnny) It's Tinker to EE-v'rs to Chance, not Tinker to EH-v'rs to Chance, the Hall-of-Fame double-play combination for the Chicago Cubs. (Joe Tinker played short, Evers second and Frank Chance first.)

excerpt (noun) EK-surpt
(verb) ik-SURPT
Definition of the noun: a former cerpt

excess ek-SES or EK-ses (ses rhymes with *yes*)

exchequer EKS-chek-'r or eks-CHEK-'r
I'm not going to stretch my little joke about
excerpt. An exchequer is not a former checker.
It's one who checks x's.

exemplary eg-ZEMP-luh-ree
Don't say: EK-zum-plair-ee or eg-ZEM-pluh-**AIR**-ee

But don't think words with the *ex* prefix never
accent the first syllable. *Exit* and *exile* are obvious
examples — make that, obvious illustrations. And
see: **exigency, exquisite** and **extant**

Exemplary means serving as a model, commend-
able. That was me (or "I," if you prefer) when I
was a jerk in Kansas City—a soda jerk, that is. I
did just fine but was fired for one little mistake. I
put an egg in a chocolate malted for the boss, Mr.
Zemp, as he asked me to do. The mistake was I
fried the egg first. Otherwise I was exemplary. And
the malt was definitely egg-ZEMP-luh-ree.

exigency EK-sih-gen-see or ek-SIJ-'n-see

exit EK-sit
Also: EG-zit

ex parte eks PAR-tay
Don't say: eks PART
Definition: one-sided

experiment ek-SPAIR-uh-m'nt
Don't say: ek-SPEER-uh-m'nt

expert (adjective) ek-SPURT or EK-spurt

expertise EK-spur-**TEEZ**
Don't say: EK-spur-**TEES** (TEES rhymes with *cease*)

A Groton listener tells me: There was this new guy working in the Parts Department. He couldn't find a thing. He spent 20 minutes looking for a franges cover for a 1926 Chandler. "I thought you told me you'd been around motors all your life," growled the boss.

The new mechanic smiled up from a tangle of nuts, bolts, coils and stuff. "Nope," he confessed, "I'm a stranger to these parts."

explicable ek-SPLIK-uh-b'l or EK-splih-kuh-b'l

exquisite ek-SKWIZ-it or EK-skwih-zit

extant EK-stint
Don't say: ek-STANT

extraordinary ek-STROR-dih-nair-ee
Don't say: EK-struh-**OR**-dih-nair-ee

If the latter sounds appropriate to your use, at least consider it as two words, and spell it as two words.

facade, façade fuh-SAHD
Don't say: fuh-KAYD

factor FAK-t'r
Don't say: FAK-tor (rhymes with *back door*)
See: **actor**

falcon FAL-kuhn (FAL rhymes with *pal* and *gal*)
Also: **FAWL-kuhn** (FAWL sounds like *fall*)

fantastic fan-TAS-tik
Some have a habit of pronouncing this word as if it were van-TAS-tik. It's not. In fact, it's quite ordinary.

farcical FAR-sik-'l
Don't say: FAR-shul

Think of bicycle—a bicycle that will take you far away–a FAR-sick-l.

February   **FEB**-roo-**AIR**-ee
No longer unacceptable: **FEB**-yoo-AIR-ee
We agree with those who leave out the *r* that February is a knotty word to say. Take your choice.

fecund   FEK-und or FEE-kund
Don't say: fuh-KUND

fertile   FUR-t'l
It's only FUR-tyl (tyl like *tile*) in Britain.
See: **docile, fragile, futile, hostile, mobile, servile, versatile** and **volatile**, as well as **domicile, juvenile** and **textile**

fete, fête   fayt (sounds like *fate*)
Avoid: fet
Definition: a festival, feast, holiday or celebration

fiat   FEE-at or FEE-aht
Also: fee-AHT

fiduciary   fih-**DOO**-shee-AIR-ee
Also: fih-DOO-shuh-ree

Fiennes, Ralph   fighns (sounds like *fines*), rayf (rhymes with *safe*) Both the first and last name of this English actor are frequently mispronounced, and the first name especially stumps Americans.

fillet   verb: fih-LAY
noun: FIL-ay or fih-LAY

Meaning slice, *fillet* is also spelled *filet*; meaning a ribbon, strip or ridge, it is pronounced FIL-it.

fission   FISH-un
Don't say: FIZH-un
Fusion is FYOO-zhun but fission is FISH-un.
See: **coercion**

flaccid FLAK-sid
Avoid: FLAS-id
See: **accelerator, accessory, succinct**

flattery Definition: when your tires are very low. You can see why they say flattery will get you nowhere!

flaunt, flout These two quite different words sound so much alike that they are often confused. To flaunt is to show off. To flout is to treat with contempt.

flummery Definition: an empty compliment, empty, trifling nonsense. For example: The introductory speech was peppered with flummeries.

foliage FOH-lee-ij
Don't say: FOHL-yij

The *ia* combination usually makes one syllable, as in *controversial, essential, potential, racial*, etc., but not in *foliage*.

forbade See: **bade**

forehead FOR-id (rhymes with *horrid*)

It sure looks like FOR-hed, and that's a so much more common pronunciation, that FOR-id is coming to seem old-fashioned.

But Longfellow's verse loses all the fun if you don't pronounce it FOR-rid:

There was a little girl
Who had a little curl
Right in the middle of her forehead;
And when she was good
She was very, very good,
But when she was bad she was horrid.

HENRY WADSWORTH LONGFELLOW

In *The King's English*, the writer Kingsley Amis said he always pronounced *forehead* FOR-rid until the sheer incomprehension of the students in a lecture class he was teaching drove him to say the hell with Longfellow's little girl. But he went only half way, giving in to "fawhed." He had an excuse. He was British.

foreign places   As Shakespeare wrote, "To anglicize or not to anglicize, that is the question." Or maybe it was my Uncle Imported who said that. The more often a foreign place is spoken of in English the more likely we are to anglicize it. Roma becomes Rome, Wien becomes Vienna, Makkah becomes Mecca. It usually sounds stilted or inappropriate in English to give such places as Quebec or Paris French pronunciations or Puerto Rico or Chile Spanish ones. Places with Spanish names that are not widely known, including many in the U.S., retain their indigenous pronunciation. See: **La Jolla** and **Ojai**

formidable   FORM-ih-dih-b'l or FOR-mih-dih-b'l
(not much difference)
Avoid: for-MIH-duh-b'l or for-MID-uh-b'l

formulae   FORM-yuh-lee
Avoid: FORM-yuh-ly (ly sounds like *lie*)

And there's nothing wrong with *formulas* for the plural of *formula* instead of *formulae*. See: **aegis, alumnae,** etc.

forte FORT
(strong point) Don't say FOR-tay unless you mean the musical
term for loud.

fortuitous for-TOO-ih-tus
See: **arduous**

*A classified ad reads: "Generous reward for lost
dog. Three legs, blind in left eye, missing right ear,
tail broken, almost deaf, answers to the name of
'Lucky.' "*

The family at the
motorcycle races,
June, 1947.

fortune See: **arduous**

fracas FRAY-kis
Don't say: FRAK-is

*"Will you tell the court what passed between you
and your wife during the quarrel?" asked the
judge. The long-suffering husband replied: "A flat-
iron, a rolling pin, six plates and a teakettle."*

fragile FRAJ-'l
It's only FRA-jyl in Britain.
See: **docile, fertile, futile, hostile, mobile, servile,
versatile** and **volatile**, as well as **domicile, juvenile**
and **textile**

fraternity, fraternize fruh-TUR-nih-tee, **FRAT**-ur-NIGHZ
(NIGHZ rhymes with *size*)

French English has imported so many French words that we don't even consider most of them as foreignisms. The French origin of *restaurant, naïve, morale* and *surveillance*, for example, is not a factor in how they are now pronounced.

Nor is the French origin of **turquoise** any longer a factor in whether one chooses to pronounce it TUR-koyz or TUR-kwoyz. For most, that choice has no more to do with the word's French origin than the choice between uh-PART-hite or uh-PART-hate, between AY-prih-kot or AP-rih-kot, or between BERN-styne or BERN-steen.

And it seems to us that the mispronunciation of **garage** as guh-RAHJ instead of guh-RAHZH has nothing to do with the word's French pronunciation either. It is not as if those who say guh-RAHJ are rebelling against what they see as an affectation to imitate French. We tend to think that they haven't even thought about how to pronounce the word. Most of these people seem to have no problem with the French *g* in **corsage, espionage, massage** and **montage**. Nor do those who are careful with the French *g* fret over having to pronounce **foliage** with a hard *g*.

If a few shun the French *g* as somehow affected, how does one explain the misguided and mistaken attempt of so many more to sound French by pronouncing the *eur* words *oor* or *yoor* (**entrepreneur, connoisseur, saboteur, auteur, raconteur, provocateur, restaurateur, hauteur, liqueur, de rigeur, voyeur**)? If only they knew that the French pronunciation of these words is simply *ur*, as in *fur, stir* and *refer*, and that the twist they give the *eur* is indeed affected but not at all French.

For some words, French effects are more problematic. **Timbre, macabre** and **Louvre** present special cases, as does **valet**. The recommended and most common pronunciation of **timbre** (TIM-bur) is fully anglicized and the close second (TAM-bur) is half anglicized. Most speakers seem to prefer the close-to-French sound of muh-KAH-bruh, if not muh-KAHB, rather than the klutsy-sounding muh-KAH-bur. Such deference probably comes from the foreign and exotic character of the word. And we dare say that no one tries to turn *Louvre* into LOO-vur and that many even prefer the authentic-sounding LOOV to LOO-vruh. Perhaps because there's also something European about a **valet**, many seem to prefer what the scholars call pseudo-French pronunciations, va-LAY or VAL-ay instead of VAL-it, which apparently sounds merely British.

What we think all of this adds up to is that there's not much value in striving for French-sounding pronunciations in what must be regarded, now, as English words. Don't worry about what you imagine the French pronunciation might be.

Phrases are another matter. Some, such as *tour de force*, present no problem because they sound the same in French or English. And some, such as *savoir faire* and *esprit de corps*, are given their French pronunciations with ease. But other French expressions are given hybrid pronunciations. For *aide-de-camp* we say AYD-d'-KAMP as the French nasal sound in camp is unfamiliar to English, but for *cause célèbre*, few are so silly as to try to say SEL-uh-BRAY. Most speakers also anglicize **Tour de France,** which barely looks French. For the name of an event like this annual bicycle race, we think it's not too hard to give a French sound to *France.* Perhaps trying too hard to make a French phrase sound French is what leads many to mispronounce **coup de grâce.** See **haute couteur**

frequent   verb: free-KWENT
adjective: FREE-kwent
See: **default, increase**

Friday   See: **-day**

fulsome   Definition: offensive to good taste, especially as being excessive, repulsive. *Fulsome* doesn't mean full, a great amount.

fungi   FUN-jigh (jigh rhymes with *eye* and *sigh*)
Never: FUN-gigh (gigh sounds like *guy*).

Fungi is the plural of *fungus*. Advice: don't be a fun guy around athlete's foot.

futile   FYOO-t'l
It's only FYOO-tyl (tyl sounding like *tile*) in Britain. See: **docile, fertile, fragile, hostile, mobile, servile, versatile** and **volatile**, as well as **domicile, juvenile** and **textile**

gabardine, gaberdine   GAB-uhr-deen
Also: gab-uhr-DEEN
Never: GARB-uh-deen

Saying it wrong can make you spell it wrong, and vice versa. A Hartford clothier advertised a sale on "garbadine" suits. The ad made us wonder if the suits were seconds, with various imperfections.

Galileo   GAL-ih-**LAY**-oh
Don't say: GAL-ih-LEE-oh

Gandhi   GAHN-dee
Avoid: GAN-dee

Many years ago Mahatma Gandhi was interviewed by reporters on a mission to London. One of them asked, "What do you think of Western Civilization?" Gandhi smiled faintly and answered, "I think it would be a very good idea."

gaol   jail
Don't say: gail

This British word means and sounds like *jail*.

garage   guh-RAHZH
Avoid: guh-RAHJ

The second *g* in garage is often called the French *g*. We also hear it in *corsage, espionage, massage* and *montage*. Don't use a French *g* in *garbage*—unless your trash is very, very fancy, nor in *foliage* or *assuage*.

garrote guh-RAHT or guh-ROHT
Avoid: GAIR-it

With Connie Mack, who became a model in longevity, managing the Philadelphia Athletics for half a century to become the all-time record holder in major league baseball wins with 3,755. Mack was in Connecticut the year after his retirement at age 87. I was master of ceremonies when Mack was honored at Hartford's Bulkeley Stadium.

geisha GAY-shuh
Avoid: GEE-shuh

Genghis GENG-gis
(Khan) Avoid: JENG-gis

genre ZHAHN-ruh
Avoid: JAHN-ruh

genuine JEN-yoo-in
Be careful of JEN-yoo-win and, worse,
JEN-yoo-ighn or JEN-yoo-wighn
(wighn sounds like *wine*).

According to my research they say JEN-yoo-ighn in Sneeb, South Carolina; Slace, Arkansas; Fleech, Montana; Grink, Utah; Borse, Louisiana; Trilb, Delaware; Mupplevalley, Kansas; Taboof, Minnesota; Plurant, New Hampshire; Sneervale, Oregon. and Whoopdedoo, Tennessee.

Gila HEE-luh
Don't say: GEE-luh.

Glastonbury   GLAS-tuhn-bair-ee
(Connecticut)   Also: **GLAS-uhn-bair-ee**

gondola   GAHN-duh-luh
Avoid: gahn-DOH-luh

government   GUHV-urn-m'nt
Don't say: GUHV-ur-m'nt. Don't forget the *n* in the middle.

Once again, three consonants in a row are not easy, but try to keep the *n* before the *m*.

A taxpayer is someone who doesn't have to pass a civil service exam to work for the government.

grandeur   GRAN-j'r
Avoid: GRAN-d'r

grand jury   I've long thought that GRAND JUR-ee is preferable to grand JUR-ee, to distinguish the phrase from *petite jury*. Phil tells me that *grand jury* can also be distinguished from *grand assize* (ah-SEEZ), the great jury instituted by Henry II and composed of sixteen knights before whom one could choose a trial in preference to trial by battle. Although *assize* means jury and could be grand or petite, one might want to say grand JUR-ee to distinguish it from the not-identical term *grand assize*. I think I'll stick with GRAND JUR-ee.

Speakers too easily forget the sense of what they're saying. How often have you been listening to a baseball game and heard something like this. The score is, say, Red Sox 2, Yankees 1. The Sox score another run and the announcer says, "That makes it three to **one**," instead of "That makes it **three** to one." When the emphasis is put in the wrong place, the listener usually doesn't know what hit him. He knows something is wrong. He has a vague sense that the announcer is just saying words rather than expressing meaning, but he doesn't notice where that feeling comes from. The result may be that his attention wanders, just as the announcer's has.

greasy GREE-see
Avoid: GREE-zee

grievous GREE-vus
Don't say: GREE-vee-us
See: **mischievous**

grimace grih-MAYS (MAYS rhymes with *face*) or GRIM-is

grocery GROH-suh-ree or GROHS-ree
Avoid: GROH-shuh-ree and GROHSH-ree

guerrilla gair-IL-uh
(first two syllables rhyme with *fair HILL*)
Also: guh-RIL-uh (same as *gorilla*)

Guglielmo gool-YEL-moh

Hartford's Willie Pep was born in Middletown, Connecticut, Guglielmo Papaleo. There never was a better boxer than Willie.

I hope fellow Radio Hall of Famer Paul Harvey didn't think I was putting him down. At our induction ceremony in Chicago in 1995, he referred to the inventor of the radio, Guglielmo Marconi, but pronounced his first name jool-YEL-moh. I felt that the audience for so dignified an occasion, both in the hall and for the radio broadcast, simply could not be left with an incorrect pronunciation of the name of radio's founding father, so when I accepted my award I pointed out that "someone" that evening had mispronounced gool-YEL-moh as jool-YEL-moh. *Giu* in Italian is pronounced *joo*, as in *Giuseppe*, but *Gu* is *goo*.

guillotine   **GIL**-uh-TEEN
Avoid: **GEE**-yuh-TEEN

Guyana   guy-AHN-uh
Avoid: gee-AHN-uh

gymnast   JIM-nast or JIM-nist

gynecologist   GY-nuh-**KAHL**-uh-jist (GY sounds like *guy*)
Do not say: JY-nuh-**KAHL**-uh-jist

halcyon HAL-see-ahn
Don't say: HAL-ee-kahn
Definition: noun, a mythical bird; adjective, calm, peaceful

Halley's (Comet) HAL-eez
Halley (Berry) HAL-ee
Don't say HAY-leez for the comet or HAY-lee for the actress.

Hambletonian HAM-b'l-**TOH**-nee-'n
Don't confuse with (Alexander) Hamiltonian.

Several months before the Hambletonian one year, I interviewed an owner of trotting horses and asked him if he was planning to race his best three-year old. "You bet I am," he replied, "and I think I can beat him."

handbook Don't say HAN-book. Many tend to leave out the *d* in this word, as well as in *handcrafted, handful, handgun, handshake, handwriting*, etc. But do leave out the *d* in *handsome* (HAN-sum); and see *handkerchief*.

handkerchief HAN-kur-chif or HANG-kur-chif
Avoid: HAN-kur-cheef and HAND-kur-chif

hara-kiri HAHR-uh-KEER-ee or HAIR-uh-KEER-ee
Better to perform hara-kiri than to pronounce it: HAIR-ee-KAIR-ee.

harass huh-RAS or HAIR-is

Hartford HART-f 'rd
Hartford, Connecticut is named after the English city of Hertford, which is pronounced HAH-f'd.

The four boys, from front to back, Steve, Phil, Paul and Robert.

haute couture oht koo-TOOR
The pronunciation of this French phrase is rarely anglicized. One can only suppose that anything less than pure French just wouldn't do for a word meaning high fashion. The *ure* of *couture* may be a culprit in the mispronuciation of words from French ending in *eur*. See the next entry.

hauteur ho-TUR or oh-TUR (TUR like *tur* in *turn*)
Never: ho-TOOR, ho-TYOOR, oh-TOOR or oh-TYOOR.
See: **connoisseur, entrepreneur** and other words from the French ending in *eur*: **amateur, saboteur, auteur, raconteur, chauffeur, provocateur, restaurateur, liqueur, de rigeur, voyeur**

"Your new overcoat is pretty loud, isn't it?"
"Yes," I replied, "but I intend to buy a muffler to go with it."

Hawaii huh-WY-ee or
hah-VAH-ee (preferred by many in Hawaii)

Two tourists were debating the pronunciation of
Hawaii as they walked down the street on their
vacation there. One said, "It's huh-WY-ee," and
the other countered, "No, I think it's huh-VY-ee."
They decided to ask the next person they met.

"Can you tell us whether this island we're on
is called hu-WY-ee or hu-VY-ee?" one asked.

"Huh-VY-ee," the man answered.

"Thank you," came the reply.

"You're velcome," said the man.

hearth harth (*th* as in *thin*–rhymes with *Darth* Vader
and *Garth* Brooks)
Don't say: hurth

height hyt (rhymes with *fight*)
Don't say: hyth
And don't spell it *heighth*. *Width,* yes. *Length,* yes.
Breadth, yes. But *heighth,* never.

Casey Stengel once told his team to "line up alphabetically according to your height."

heinous HAY-nus
Don't say: HY-nus or HEE-nus

Heisman HYZ-m'n
(Trophy) Don't say: HYS-m'n

Helena HEL-uh-nuh
(Montana) Don't say: huh-LAY-nuh or huh-LEE-nuh

helicopter **HEL**-ih-KAHP-t'r
Don't say: **HEE**-luh-KAHP-t'r

Helsinki HEL-sing-kee
(Finland) Don't say: hel-SING-kee

herb, herbal urb, UR-b'l
British: hurb, HUR-b'l
But sound the *h* in *herbicide* and *herbivore*.

While words beginning with a silent *h* are preceded by *an* instead of *a* (*an herb, an honor*), some overdo this principle by improperly extending it to words in which an initial *h* is sounded. Don't say: *an hotel, an hundred years.*

herculean, hur-KYOO-lee-in or HUR-kyoo-**LEE**-in
Herculean Definition: having unusual strength or stamina or unusual difficulty

heterogeneity HET-uh-roh-juh-**NEE**-ih-tee
Don't say: HET-uh-roh-juh-**NAY**-ih-tee
See: **deity, homogeneity, simultaneity, spontaneity**

Heublein After the first members of Connecticut's famous Heublein family immigrated from Germany, they began pronouncing their name HIGH-blighn instead of the traditional German HOY-blighn.

Then, some years back, the Heublein distilling and related enterprise decided to change the pronunciation of the business name to HYOO-blighn.

Himalaya HIM-uh-LAY-uh or hih-MAHL-'-yuh

The mountain climber's guide warned, "Don't slip. It's an 8,000-foot drop. But if you do, look to the left. It's a terrific view!"

Holyoke
(Massachusetts)

HOHL-yohk (sounds like *whole yolk*)
Don't say: HOH-lee-OHK
Just remember, there are lots of oaks in Holyoke, but not a single one is holy.

holocaust, Holocaust **HAHL**-uh-KAWST
Don't say: **HOH**-luh-KAWST or **HAWL**-uh-KAWST

hosiery HOH-zhuh-ree
Don't say: HOHZ-uh-ree

The boy's mother demanded, "I want you to put on a fresh pair of socks every day." He promised he would and did as he promised. By the end of two weeks he couldn't get his shoes on.

homage HAHM-ij or AHM-ij

homicide HAHM-ih-syd
Avoid: HOH-mih-syd

Reginald Dewar, a big game hunter from Glastonbury, has been missing for two weeks. It is feared that something he disagreed with ate him.

homogeneity HOH-muh-juh-**NEE**-ih-tee
Don't say: HOH-muh-juh-**NAY**-ih-tee
See: **deity, heterogeneity, simultaneity, spontaneity**

homogeneous HOH-muh-**JEE**-nee-us
Don't confuse with *homogenous* (huh-MAHJ-uh-nus), a word very similar in meaning. While *homogeneous* means alike or uniform in nature, structure, kind or quality, *homogenous* is chiefly a biological term meaning similar because of common descent or origin, exhibiting homogeny—the correspondence between body parts or organs of organisms which may have different functions but common descent. Many mispronounce *homogeneous* as if it were *homogenous*.

hopefully Although many object to the dangling use of *hopefully*, as in, "Hopefully, the recession will be over soon," the objection on grammatical grounds seems fussy. We think the more important issue is that hopefully is evasive and over-used. Writer Kingsley Amis only slightly overstates it when he comments that such a use shows us "immediately that we are dealing with a dimwit at best." As Amis goes on to say, the real problem with hopefully is that it is dishonest, a favorite with waffling politicians, putting on "a false show of nearly promising something while actually saying precious little."

hors d'oeuvres or DURVZ

hospitable hah-SPIT-uh-b'l or HAHS-pit-uh-b'l

hostile HAHS-t'l
British: HAHS-tyl (tyl sounds like *tile*).

hotelier hoh-tel-YAY
Don't say: hoh-tel-YUR, hoh-TEL-yur, or hoh-TEL-ee-ur. *Hotelier* is not pronounced like **clothier**.
Definition: owner or proprietor of a hotel

Houston
(Texas)
HYOO-stun
Watch out for YOO-stun. Get that *h* in there. The same goes for *huge* and *human*.

Same pronunciation for Sam Houston, one of the founders of Texas, from whom the city got its name, and performing artist Whitney Houston.

huge
hyooj
Don't say: yooj

Just as you can get away with pronouncing many *wh* words without the aspirated *h* (see: **wail, whale**), so you can get by with pronouncing many *hu* words without it. Saying *human, humanity, humid, humor* and even *humiliate* as if they began with *y* is hardly illiterate or vulgar, but some words and names seem especially deserving of the extra effort, such as *huge, hue, hubris, Hugo, Hugh* and *Hughes*. Escape artist Harry Houdini, not an *hu* word, is hoo-DEE-nee, not hyoo-DEE-nee.

hygienic,
hygienist
high-JEN-ik, high-JEN-ist
Avoid: high-jee-EN-ik, high-jee-EN-ist

The *i* is not wasted. If you note that it serves to soften the *g* into a *j* sound, you may feel less compelled to sound the *i* just because it's there. See **arduous, egregious**.

I and me   Many otherwise well-spoken people mar their speech by not knowing when to use *I* and when to use *me*. The most common error is to use I after a transitive verb or a preposition. This is a mistake because transitive verbs and prepositions turn personal pronouns (*I, he, she, we, they*) into direct objects and require the speaker to switch to the pronoun's objective form (*me, him, her, us, them*).

Don't say: Bill called Jim and I into his office.
Say: Bill called Jim and me into his office.

Don't say: This is just between you and I.
Say: This is just between you and me.

Don't say: Are you coming with Jim and I?
Say: Are you coming with Jim and me?

This was a camera test for Channel 3, WTIC's new venture in 1957. We reprised "Strictly Sports," added photos and film and called it "Close-Up on Sports." WTIC radio and WTIC-TV split when the Travelers sold the stations in 1975. We moved to the Gold Building on Main Street and the TV became WFSB.

Iacocca IGH-uh-**KOH**-kuh

Although he won't discuss it, Lee Iacocca's original family name was not Iacocca, but just plain old Cocca. Apparently the Coccas arrived in the United States late in the 1840s, and settled in Maine. That's where they picked up the I-a.

iced tea William Safire has pointed out that we usually don't pronounce the *d* in *iced tea*, *baked potato* or *queen-sized bed*, or the *ed* in *damned lies*, *corned beef* or *whipped cream*, but we should still spell these words and write them in full. At least, until they reach the status of *skim milk* (no longer *skimmed milk*), *cream cheese* (no longer *creamed cheese*) and *popcorn* (no longer *popped corn*). A similar process turns *cut and dried* into *cut and dry*. See **catty-cornered**.

ideology EYE-dee-**AHL**-uh-jee or ID-ee-**AHL**-uh-jee

Illinois IL-ih-**NOY** (rhymes with *little boy*)
Don't say: IL-ih-**NOYZ**

During peace negotiations with Lincoln and Secretary of State Seward, Confederate Vice President Alexander Stephens told a story about Illinois. When that state came into the union, he said, no one knew how to pronounce it. Illinoy or Illinoyz? John Quincy Adams, Stephens told his adversaries, came up with the quip, "If one were to judge from the character of the representatives in this Congress from that state, I should decide unhesitatingly that the proper pronunciation was *Allnoise*." See: **Iroquois**

illogical pronunciations **victuals, business, mortgage, comptroller, laboratory, Wednesday, viscount,** *chocolate,* **colonel,** *woman/women*

imbroglio   im-BROHL-yoh
Don't say: im-BRO-glee-oh or im-BRO-lee-oh
Definition: a complicated, confusing or difficult situation

immature   See: **mature**

impeccable   A woodpecker finds an iron telephone pole *impeccable*.

impious   IM-pee-us
Less acceptable: im-PY-us (PY sounds like *pie*)

imply, infer   Just as there's a big difference between *inflict* and *suffer* (think of a punishment), so there's an important difference between *imply* and *infer*. If the prosecutor implied that the witness was lying, he suggested it. If he inferred that the witness was lying, he concluded as much from the testimony.

This distinction is important, but the misuse of *infer* to mean *imply* is so common that some dictionaries have nonetheless recognized it. We urge keeping a clear distinction, for two reasons. First, if the distinction is lost, how will you know what's meant if someone writes or says that the prosecutor inferred the witness was lying? Or, if someone writes that the President inferred that a political opponent intends to run against him? Second, *infer* is used in place of *imply* by people who think it means "imply" in order to use a less common word, a word they ironically believe makes them sound more educated. This misuse is much like the substitution of "between you and I" for the correct "between you and me" or the misapplication of *disinterested* to mean merely uninterested or bored instead of without bias or interest.

in absentia ab-SEN-shuh or ab-SEN-shee-uh
not: ab-SENT-shuh
nor: ab-STEN-shuh (probably confused with abstention)
nor: ab-SEN-chuh
nor: ab-SEN-tee-uh

inchoate in-KOH-it
Don't say: in-KOH-ate
Definition: just begun, at an early stage

incidentally IN-sih-**DENT**-'l-ee
Don't say: IN-sih-**DENT**-lee. Sound all five syllables, not just four. Most people have no difficulty giving adjectives ending in *al* an additional syllable when *ly* is added for the adverb form: e.g. *traditionally, informally, nationally*. But some will shorten *finally* to two syllables, and *especially, generally, usually, actually* and *naturally* to three, leaving out the *al* when they should not. For a few adjectives ending in *ic*—such as *specific* and *ironic*, however, the *al* in the adverb form is properly silenced. *Specifically* and *ironically* should be pronounced in four syllables, not five.

incognito   IN-kahg-**NEE**-toh or in-KAHG-nih-toh

incomparable   See: **comparable**

incongruous   in-KAHNG-groo-us
Don't say: IN-kahn-GROO-us

increase   A great many two-syllable words that double as nouns and verbs shift the stress from the first to the second syllable and vice versa as their use changes. (Some longer words also follow this pattern, e.g. *attribute*.) *Increase* as a noun is IN-krees and as a verb it's in-KREES. When you say you want to IN-krees production or that you're reporting an in-KREES, you may be understood, but you're throwing off your listener, distracting him or her from the point of what you're trying to say. It may seem like a small thing, but sometimes small things can make a big difference. See: **default, baptize, contrasting, English**

indefatigable   IN-dih-**FAT**-ih-guh-b'l
Never say: IN-dih-fuh-**TEEG**-uh-b'l

Indian   IN-dee-'n

Lake Chargoggagoggmanchaugagogchaubuna-gunggamaug in Massachusetts, by the way, is pronounced just the way it looks. I understand that it translates as "You fish on your side, we'll fish on our side, and nobody fish in the middle."

My last boxing bout was against one Chief Adams, an Indian from Oklahoma. He wasn't really a chief. He was old enough to be one, but not smart enough. He had been banged around by every bum in the Midwest and couldn't bruise an over-ripe eggplant with his Sunday punch, and if he was nicked on the arm by a cream puff, he'd hit the canvas like a safe falling down an elevator shaft. He won an eight-round decision over me, and I had HAD it!

indict   in-DIGHT (DIGHT rhymes with *white*)
The *c* is silent in *indict* but not in *interdict* (IN-tur-**DIKT**)

inexorable   in-EK-sur-uh-b'l
Don't say: IN-ek-**SOR**-uh-b'l

inexplicable   in-EK-splih-kuh-b'l – if you can get it out of your mouth. Such tongue twisters justify going with something easier: IN-ek-**SPLIH**-kuh-b'l. Likewise for *inextricable*, but **inexorable** (in-EK-sur-uh-b'l) you should be able to handle.

infamous   IN-fuh-mus
Don't say: in-FAY-mus

infiltrate   in-FIL-trayt or IN-fil-trayt

inflammable   *Flammable* and *inflammable* alike mean easily set on fire. The in prefix of *inflammable* misleads some into thinking it means the opposite of *flammable*, or hard to set on fire–a mistake that could, of course, be quite serious. The opposite of *flammable* and *inflammable* is *noninflammable* or, preferably, *nonflammable*, which like non- compounds generally, does not take a hyphen.

influence   IN-floo-ints
Don't say: in-FLOO-ints
The pronunciation is the same for the noun and the verb.

ingenuous, ingenious   Don't confuse *ingenuous* (free from reserve or dissimulation) with *ingenious*. And don't misspell *ingenious* as *ingenius*.

in half The phrase *in half* may be justified as idiomatic, but we prefer the more precise *in halves*. No matter how carefully I measure, I've never been able to cut anything in two and end up with just onc half.

inherent in-HEER-int
Watch out for: in-HAIR-int

ingenue **AN**-zhuh-NOO
Don't say: **AHN**-zhuh-NOO

innovative **IN**-noh-VAY-t'v
Don't say: IN-noh-**VAY**-t'v or IN-oh-vuh-t'v

innuendo

Beware of burglars. If you don't lock up, one may come innuendo.

inquiry in-KWYR-ee or IN-kwi-ree

integral IN-tuh-grul
Don't say: in-TEG-rul
Death penalty: IN-truh-gul
Just look at the spelling!

interesting IN-tris-ting or IN-tur-uh-sting or
IN-tur-ES-ting
Avoid: IN-tris-teen
Don't say: **IN**-ur-ES-ting

intravenous IN-truh-**VEE**-nus
Don't say: IN-truh-VEE-nee-us

intrepid in-TREP-id
Don't say: IN-truh-pid

Iran ih-RAHN or ee-RAHN or eye-RAN

Iraq ih-RAHK or eye-RAK

Iroquois **EER**-uh-KWOY (EER rhymes with *ear*,
KWOY with *toy*)
Don't say: **EER**-uh-KOY, **EER**-uh-KWAH or
EER-uh-KOYS. See: **Illinois**

irregardless *Irregardless* is substandard. If you're not content
with *regardless*, why not go all the way to *disirre-*
gardless? The negative prefix cancels the negative
suffix, leaving the poor word in a helluvafix!
Pulling all guards out of Erie, Pennsylvania, left
Erie guardless.

irreparable ih-REP-ur-uh-b'l
Don't say: EER-ree-**PAIR**-uh-b'l

irrevocable ih-REV-uh-kuh-b'l
Don't say: EER-ree-**VOH**-kuh-b'l

isthmus IS-mus
As in **asthma,** the *th* is silent.

Italian ih-TAL-yun
Don't say: EYE-tal-yun

A Hartford delicatessen owner was called in to
review his income tax return. "I slave all day to
make a living for my wife and two sons," he complained to the IRS agent, "and you question my
measly $7,000 income. Why?"
Agent: "It's not your income tax we question. It's
the six trips you made to Italy last year, which you
deducted as a business expense."
Deli owner: "Oh, that, I forgot to tell you–we also
deliver."

Japanese JAP-uh-**NEES** or JAP-uh-**NEEZ**
See: Chinese and Portuguese

Show me a man who comes home in the evening, is greeted by a smile, is encouraged to take off his shoes, has pillows arranged on the floor for him, and is served a delicious meal—and I'll show you a man who lives in a Japanese restaurant.

jewelry JOO-'l-ree
JOOL-ree is close enough.
Never say: JOO-luh-ree

jodhpurs JAHD-purz
Definition: a style of riding breeches loose above the knees and tight below.

jubilation JOO-bih-**LAY**-sh'n
Don't say: JOO-byoo-**LAY**-sh'n

judgment Don't spell it *judgement* unless you're in Britain.

judiciary joo-DISH-ee-air-ee
Watch out for: joo-DISH-ur-ee
See: **beneficiary** and **subsidiary**, and **penitentiary** and **auxiliary**

Juliet JOOL-y'ht or JOOL-ee-'ht
Avoid: JOOL-ee-ET

In speaking of "Romeo and Juliet" many seem to find it natural, perhaps even romantic, to stress the third syllable in *Juliet* to balance the stress of the third syllable in Romeo, proving perhaps that not all natural inclinations are to be encouraged. Don't confuse *Juliet* with *Juliette*.

juror JOOR-ur
Don't say: JOOR-or

Looking at the jury, the judge angrily asked:
"What possible excuse can you give for acquitting this man?"
"Insanity, your honor," replied the foreman.
"All twelve of you?" cried the judge.

juvenile JOO-vuh-n'l or JOO-vuh-nyl (nyl sounds like *Nile*)

The British JOO-vuh-nyl is common in American English. But see: **fertile, fragile, futile, hostile, mobile, servile, versatile** and **volatile**. Note that not all words ending in *-ile* follow this pattern: e.g. *exile, senile,* and some, such as **domicile** and **textile**, are commonly heard with either the American short *i* or the British long *i*.

A marble tournament was in full swing. Little Johnny missed an easy shot and in a loud voice uttered a real cuss word. A preacher who was among the spectators called to him: "Johnny, what happens to little boys who swear? Replied little Johnny, "They grow up to be golfers."

juvenilia JOO-vuh-**NIL**-ee-uh
See: **memorabilia**

Kabul KAH-b'l (rhymes with *hobble* and *bobble*)
(Afghanistan) Don't say: kah-BOOL

kaffiyeh ka-FEE-yuh
Definition: a headdress consisting of a rectangular
cloth fastened by a cord around the crown, often
worn by Arab men in parts of the Near East,
cousin to the fez and turban. The cord is
an ekal.

kamikaze KAH-mih-**KAH**-zee

karaoke KAIR-ee-**OH**-kee
Avoid: kuh-ROH-kee

khaki KAK-ee (rhymes with *wacky*)
Avoid: KAH-kee

kibosh KY-bahsh or kih-BAHSH
Definition: something that stops: put the kibosh
on that idea.

kilometer KIL-uh-**MEE**-t'r
Avoid: kih-LAHM-ih-t'r
Say the *kilo* in *kilometer* as you would *kilo* in
kilogram and *kilowatt*.

The metric system helped me lose weight.
Overnight I went down from 201 to 92.

kimono kih-MOH-nuh
Also: kih-MOH-noh

A sign in a store in California that sells kimonos and other novelties says, "Kimono my house."

kindergarten **KIN**-dur-GAHRT-'n or **KIN**-dur-GARD-'n
Don't say: **KIN**-duh-GARD-'n or
KIN-dee-GARD-'n

A kindergarten teacher in Longmeadow was instructing the youngsters in her class as to proper classroom etiquette. "If anyone must go to the bathroom during the day, please raise your hand," the teacher requested. "How will that help?" asked one of her students.

Ku Klux Klan KOO-kluhks-**KLAN**
Don't say: KLOO-kluhks-**KLAN**

kudos KOO-dahs (rhymes with *MS-DOS* and *Haas*, as in golfer Jay Haas)
Not as good: KYOO-dahs, KYOO-dohs, KYOO-dohz, KOO-dohs, KOO-dohz

Anyone who uses a word like *kudos*, instead of something simpler such as *praise*, should take care in its pronunciation. Its users should also use it correctly. Just as *pathos* is not a plural form of *patho*, the *s* does not make *kudos* a plural and there is no such thing as a single *kudo*–at least not yet.

Kuwait k'-WAYT or koo-WAYT

Kyff kighf (rhymes with *knife*)
(Rob) Rob Kyff writes the nationally syndicated column "Word Watch," which appears in the Hartford Courant.

L

laboratory   **LAB**-ruh-**TOR**-ee
Also: **LAB**-uh-ruh-**TOR**-ee
Never say: **LAB**-ur-TOR-ee
British: luh-BOR-uh-tree.

labyrinthine   LAB-uh-**RIN**-thin
LAB-uh-**RIN**-theen
LAB-uh-**RIN**-thyn (thyn rhymes with *wine*).

lackadaisical   LACK-uh-**DAY**-zih-k'l
Never ever say: LAX-uh-**DAY**-zih-k'l

Since a person who's *lackadaisical* about something
might also be described as *lax*, many lackadaisical
speakers are deceived into the LAX-uh-DAY-zih-k'l
mispronunciation. There's also probably some
attraction in the softer *x* sound instead of the
harsher *k* sound.

The following is a transcription from a recording
of The Bob Steele Show on WTIC-AM 1080 on
November 4, 1988:

"Would you believe that S. Daniel Giuliani of
West Hartford writes about the word lackadaisical,
which we had recently — he says, 'You said that
you hadn't used the word in a couple of years. I
want to give you some facts here,' and he lists the
times and the dates on which I used the word
lackadaisical, which, incidentally, is mispronounced LAX-uh-day-zih-k'l, now and then, in
case you missed it the first time. Anyway, he says
Monday, October 31, 1988–that was the last time,

and Friday, August 21, 1987, January 15, 1987, February 19, 1986, September 5, 1985, December 12, 1984, May 27, 1983, December 31, 1982, March 12, 1982, October 28, 1981 and August 17, 1981. That's exactly what he has written down here, and I wouldn't argue with Dan, because he keeps track of these words. Didn't realize I'd used that so often, but anyway, we're sure to hit somebody with it for the first time, no matter how many times we use it. Well, there are only so many words, over the years, you take fifty years, six days a week, or five days a week, five words a week, how many words is that in 50 years? Got to repeat 'em now and then."

In an interview in 1950 with former world heavy-weight champion Gene Tunney, I asked about the controversial "long count" in his 1927 rematch with Jack Dempsey. Tunney had gotten up to retain the title, after referee Dave Barry delayed the count until he got Dempsey into a neutral corner. While Tunney told me the count made no difference, Dempsey (on the right), interviewed for "Strictly Sports" a few years later, told me Tunney had the better case.

La Guardia   luh-GWAHR-dee-uh
Don't say: luh GAHR-dee-uh

laissez-faire   LEH-say-FAIR
Avoid: LEH-zay-**FAIR** or LAY-say-**FAIR**
or LAY-zay-**FAIR**

La Jolla luh-HOY-uh (HOY rhymes with *toy* and *boy*)
(California) Don't say: luh JAHL-uh

When our pioneer ancestors began running out of, or growing out of, English and other European names to give to their communities (Plymouth, Jamestown, New Amsterdam, New Haven, New London, Charleston, etc.), there were plenty of native American ones available (e.g. Naugatuck, Chicopee, Milwaukee, Saginaw, Connecticut, Mississippi). They were also fond of classical names (Syracuse, Troy, Utica, Athens, Sparta, etc.). English-speaking settlers had little allegiance to Old World pronunciations when they founded places like Coventry, Connecticut and Valparaiso, Indiana. Not being from Egypt, those who created Cairo, Illinois anglicized the pronunciation to KAY-roh. After English-speaking migrants got to Nouvelle Orlèans, a pronunciation struggle went on for decades, resulting in multiple ways to say **New Orleans**. But when the gringos got to places like San Diego, San Jose and La Jolla, the pronunciation of the Americans already there, mostly of Spanish and native American descent, was so well-established that it was never anglicized, and in other places, such as Los Angeles, only slightly so.

lamentable luh-MEN-t'-b'l
Or, if you can say it without suffering lockjaw, LAM-'n-tuh-b'l. You'll know you're right if you say LAM-'n-tuh-b'l, but luh-MEN-t'-b'l is forgivable. See: **applicable, formidable, inexplicable**

languor LAYN-gur (rhymes with *anger*)
Don't say: LAYN-gwur

larvae LAHR-vee
Don't say: LAHR-vy (vy sounds like *vie*, rhymes with *tie*) See: **alumnae, antennae, vertebrae**

larynx LAIR-ingks
Watch out for: LAHR-nix
Look at the spelling and you should say it right,
and vice versa.

lascivious luh-SIV-ee-us
Don't say: luh-SHIV-ee-us

lasso LAS-oh
Avoid: las-SOO

laundry LAWN-dree
Don't say: LAWN-dur-ee

lead, led No one has a problem pronouncing *led*, the past
tense of *lead*, but, confusing it with the noun *lead*,
many misspell it *lead*.

LeFleur, Guy GEE luh-FLUR (luh as in *look*, FLUR to rhyme
with *fur*)
Don't rhyme the Canadian hockey great with
sewer. See: **connoisseur**

length lengkth
Don't say: lenth
See: **strength**

lever LEV-ur
Like many British pronunciations, LEE-vur is
preferred in some parts of the U.S., especially in
the South.

liaison lee-AY-zahn, LEE-ay-ZAHN or LEE-uh-ZAHN

library LY-brair-ee
Never say: LY-berry

We don't mind silencing the *r* in *February*, but as
the difficulty of sounding *library* with the *r* is not
even close, our ears find *LY-berry* very offensive.

Mark Twain had an overflowing library. When a close friend commented about the lack of shelf space and the dozens of books stacked on desks and windowsills, the great wit remarked: "Well, you know how difficult it is to borrow book cases?"

licorice LIK-ur-ish or LIK-ur-is

liege leej (rhymes with *siege*)
Don't say: leezh
Definition: a feudal lord entitled to allegiance

Lima LY-muh
(Ohio) But in Peru: LEE-muh

lingerie lan-zheh-REE or LAN-zheh-ree (lan as in *land*)
Don't say: LAHN-zhuh-ray or lahn-zhuh-RAY

liqueur lih-KUR
Never say: lih-KOOR, lih-KYOOR or luh-KOOR
See: **connoisseur, entrepreneur** and other words from the French ending in *eur*: **amateur, saboteur, auteur, raconteur, chauffeur, provocateur, restaurateur, hauteur, de rigeur, voyeur**

literature LIT-ur-uh-CHUR
Avoid: LIH-truh-CHOOR

The Yale freshman had gone to sleep in English class and the professor threw a book at him. "What hit me?" he asked, startled. "That," said the professor, "was a flying Chaucer."

lithe lyth (rhymes with *writhe* and *tithe*)
Don't say: lyth (like the *th* in *Smith*—rhymes with *Smythe*). See: **blithe**

loam lohm
Don't say: loom

loath lohth (rhymes with *oath*)
Don't confuse with the verb *loathe* in which the *th* sounds like the *th* in *bathe* and *writhe*. If you're *loath*, you're unwilling; if you *loathe* something, you despise it.

And don't let the difference between *loath* and *loathe* confuse you about the pronunciation of *loathsome*, in which the *loath* is pronounced like *loathe* even though it's spelled like *loath*.

log lawg
Also: lahg

loge lozh
Don't say: lohj
Definition: a theater box or the front section of a theater's mezzanine.

longevity lahn-JEV-ih-tee
Don't say: lawng-JEV-ih-tee. Don't be fooled by the *long* in *longevity*.

long-lived lawng-LYVD (rhymes with *thrived* and *arrived*)
British: lawng-LIVD (as in *outlived*)

lore A statute, rule or regulation in the state of Rhode Island. Example: speeding is against the lore.

lorgnette   lorn-YET
Definition: a pair of eyeglasses with a long handle; opera glasses

Louisiana   loo-EEZ-ee-**AN**-uh
Don't say: **LOOZ**-ee-AN-uh

Louisville   LOO-uh-vul in Louisville.
(Kentucky)   Elsewhere you can say: LOO-ee-vil

How is the capital of Kentucky pronounced? If you said LOO-uh-vul, your answer is incorrect. It's FRANK-fort.

lour, lower   LOW-er (rhymes with *hour* and *power*, not *rower* or *moviegoer*)
Definition: to scowl. One who looks angry, sullen or threatening is said to lower. Media weather forecasters sometimes speak of the clouds lowering, but pronounce it incorrectly, as if they meant that fog were descending.

Louvre   LOOV or LOO-vruh

luxury   LUHK-shuh-ree
Also: LUHG-zhuh-ree

My son Phil, testing the patience of Yogi Berra at the Yankees training camp in Fort Lauderdale in 1962, when Phil was writing for his high school paper, The Wethersfield *Post*, and the *Courant*. Phil asked Yogi if he really said, "It's not over until it's over"; and "Baseball is 90 percent mental, the other half is physical." Answered Yogi, "I never said most of the things I said."

macabre   muh-KAH-bruh (rhymes with *candelabra*) or
muh-KAHB
Avoid: muh-KAH-bur

machination   MAK-ih-**NAY**-sh'n
Don't say: MASH-ih-**NAY**-sh'n

Mackinac   MAK-uh-naw
Mackinac is the name of the strait between the
upper and lower peninsulas of Michigan which
connects Lake Huron and Lake Michigan. If you
don't get this pronunciation right, you may end
up like a listener who insists that a mackinac is a
guy who fixes cars. *Mackinac* is pronounced the
same as *Mackinaw*–the spelling for the coat, boat
and blanket.

maintenance   MAYN-tuh-nints
Don't say: MAYNT-nints

malingerer   muh-LING-g'r-'r
Don't say: muh-LIN-j'r-ër

mangrove   MANG-grohv
Avoid: MAN-grohv
The first syllable sounds the same as the first
syllable in *manganese, mangle* and *mango*.

maraschino   MAIR-uh-**SKEE**-noh
Don't say: MAIR-uh-**SHEE**-noh

marked mahrkt
Never: MAHR-kid

Don't let the three-syllable *markedly* fool you into pronouncing marked with two syllables, like *markedly* without the *ly*. See: **alleged** and **supposed**

Mark Twain It doesn't quite sound right to call him just "Twain." Better to use the full pen name of Sam Clemens, or call him Clemens.

Some of our favorite Mark Twain one-liners:

• *Wagner's music is better than it sounds.*

• *I didn't attend the funeral, but I sent a nice letter saying that I approved of it.*

• *It is curious that physical courage should be so common in the world and moral courage so rare.*

• *The best way to cheer yourself is to try to cheer someone else up.*

marquis, marquise mahr-KEE or MAHR-kwiss, mar-KEEZ
Definition: a nobleman ranking above an earl or count and below a duke. His wife (after whom the ring and the gem are named) is a marquise: mar-KEEZ

Martì, Josè mar-TEE
The accent marks over the ì in Martì and the è in Josè, unlike most accent marks, indicate stress rather than the vowel's sound. Without the accent mark, Marti would be MAHR-tee. See: **Dalì**

Phil and I visited Havana in 1960 to verify the pronunciation of the Josè Martì airport. Martì (1853-1895) was a Cuban statesman, poet and journalist. Okay, we did take in the sights as well.

Massachusetts MAS-uh-**CHOO**-sits
Don't say: MAS-uh-**CHOO**-zits

massage   muh-SAHZH
Don't say: muh-SADJ
See: **garage, corsage, espionage, sabotage, montage.**

mathematics   MATH-uh-**MAT**-ix
Don't say: math-MAT-ix
Pronounce all four syllables.

Save a dime here and a dime there, and before you know it, you'll have twenty cents.

mature   muh-TOOR or muh-CHOOR
The syllable *-ture* has yet another pronunciation–*chur*–in such words as *furniture, fixture, mixture* and *overture.*

When fruit is mature it's ripe. When it's overture, it's rotten.

mauve   mohv (rhymes with *stove* and *grove*)
Don't say: mawv

mayoral   MAY-ur-'l
Don't say: may-OR-'l
The noun, *mayoralty,* is MAY-ur-'l-tee, not

MAY-ur-**AL**-ih-tee. If you have trouble pronouncing this one–May-er-'l-tee is a tough one with all those unemphasized middle syllables–you can at least use it correctly. That is, use it only as a noun, never as an adjective:

Wrong: Jones won the mayoralty race.
Right: Jones won the mayoralty.
Right: Jones won the mayoral race.

mea culpa   MEE-uh KUL-puh

medieval   MEE-dee-**EE**-vul or MEH-dee-**EE**-vul
Avoid: mee-DEE-vul
Medieval has four syllables, not three.

In the Middle Ages when entertainers were scarce, many a king hired short, pint-sized jesters because they realized that half an oaf is better than none!

Melbourne   MEL-burn
(Australia)   Don't say: MEL-born

melee, mîlèe   MAY-lay

memento   muh-MEN-toh
Never say: moh-MEN-toh. Think of *memory*, not *moment*.

memorabilia MEM-uh-ruh-**BIL**-ee-uh or
MEM-uh-ruh-**BIL**-yuh (BIL as in Wild Bill)
Don't say: MEM-uh-ruh-**BEEL**-ee-uh or
MEM-uh-ruh-**BEEL**-yuh
Don't be misled by *automobile*.

mentor MEN-tur or MEN-tor

merchandise **MUR**-chin-DYZ
Avoid: **MUR**-chin-DYS (rhymes with *urchin dice*)
Never gamble with merchandise.

meteorologist MEE-tee-ur-**AHL**-uh-jist
Watch out for: MEE-tur-**AHL**-uh-jist.

The root is *meteor*, not *meter*. A MEE-tur-**AHL**-
uh-jist might help you find a parking space but
wouldn't know anything about the weather.

mezzo MET-soh or MEZ-oh

Michelin MEE-sh'l-in

minestrone MIN-ih-**STROH**-nee
Don't say: MIN-ih-**STROHN**
Definition: a very small cup of soup

miniature MIN-ee-uh-chur or MIN-ih-chur

minuscule mih-NUH-skyool or MIN-uh-skyool

minutia, mih-NOO-she-uh, mih-NOO-shee-ee
minutiae Avoid: mih-NOO-shuh for either singular or
plural *Minutia* has four syllables, not three.

We're tempted to leave out this entry, but not all
small details are unimportant. The plural, *minutiae* (mih-NOO-shee-ee), is often mispronounced as
if it were the singular, *minutia*. Usually the plural
is meant (small, unimportant details) and should

be spelled and pronounced accordingly. See:
alumnae, larvae, vertebrae

mischievous MIS-chih-vus
Never say: mis-CHEE-vee-us

The culprit here is the letter *e*. It doesn't figure in
the pronunciation, but many see it and just can't
let it go to waste, saying the *chiev* in the middle of
the word like that in *achievement* or the *iev* in
such words as *believe, relieve* and *grieve*. But they
don't stop there, also transposing the *e* to follow
the *v* and come up with mis-CHEE-vee-us. Even
some Ph.D.'s make this very sloppy mistake.
See: **grievous**

misogamy mih-SAHG-uh-mee
Don't say: mih-SAHJ-uh-mee

*Marriage teaches you loyalty, forbearance, self-
restraint, meekness—and a lot of other qualities
you wouldn't need if you stayed single.*

misogyny mih-SAHJ-uh-nee
Don't say: mih-SAHG-uh-nee

It may seem inconsistent to pronounce a hard *g* in
misogamy and a soft *g* in *misogyny*. We could get
into a long, technical explanation for this differ-

ence. We could, that is, if we knew the long, technical explanation.

Missouri mih-ZOOR-ee or (for old-time Missourians) mih-ZOOR-uh

I was born in Kansas City, Missouri, which borders Kansas City, Kansas. No one knows for sure why Kansas and Arkansas aren't pronounced alike, but I can tell you that Kansas is a lot different from either Arkansas or Missouri. They say it's so flat in Kansas that if your dog runs away, you can watch him for three days.

mobile MOH-b'l
(adjective) British: MOH-byl (*byl* sounds like *bile*).
See: **docile, domicile, fertile, fragile, futile, hostile, juvenile, servile, textile, versatile** and **volatile**

Mobile MOH-beel
(Alabama) Don't say: moh-BEEL or MOH-byl or MOH-bil

modernity moh-DUR-nih-tee
Don't say: moh-DAIR-nih-tee

modicum MAH-d'-kum
Don't say: MOH-d'-kum

monarch MAHN-urk or MAHN-ark
Avoid: MAHN-ARK

Monday See: **-day**

mongooses The plural of *mongoose* is not *mongeese*.
See: **perplexing plurals**

montage mohn-TAZH or mahn-TAZH
Don't say: mohn-TADJ
See: **garage, corsage, espionage, sabotage, massage**

moot   moot (rhymes with *boot*)
Don't say: myoot (rhymes with *mute*)

Moscow   MAH-skoh or MAHS-kow

moths   mawthz (th as in *the*)

In the singular, *moth*, the *th* sounds like the *th* in *math*, but it changes in the plural.

This moth and his mate had come upon a discarded pair of all-wool pearl buttoned spats and proceeded to stuff themselves, finishing one but being too uncomfortable to partake of the other. Mr. Moth took a little flight to ease his fullness and ran into an old friend who greeted him with "Hiya, Joe! Howya feelin'?" To which Joe replied, "Not so hot. Just had a spat with the wife."

I told Muhammed Ali how to beat Joe Frazier in the 1971 "Fight of the Century." Ali lost, but four years later, I kept quiet and he beat Smokin' Joe in the "Thrilla in Manila."

Muhammad   moo-HAM-id
Muhammed   moo-HAM-id
Mohammad   moh-HAM-id

All three spellings for the founder of Islam are commonly used. The spelling used by both the last name of the Nation of Islam founder and the first name of the great heavyweight boxing champion is *Muhammad*.

multi-   Unlike *anti-* and *semi-*, and sometimes *quasi-*, the *i* in this prefix is pronounced *uh* or *ih* more often than *ee*, and it's rarely *igh*.

muse, Muse   myooz

Don't say myoos, often heard for *Muse*.

Definitions: to muse is to reflect or meditate; a Muse is any of the nine daughters of Zeus who presided over the arts; inspiration.

museum   myoo-ZEE-um

Don't say: MYOO-zee-um

mythomania   MITH-oh-**MAY**-nee-uh

Definition: an abnormal propensity for lying and exaggerating

names   When it comes to people's names, spelling doesn't always seem to make a difference. In Kentucky, there's a family named Enroughty. They pronounce it Darby!

Speaking of names, have you ever noticed the confusion it can cause for some people when they have to say their name, with last name first? For example:

John Pope
Alec Smart
John King
T. Tutor
Candy Rock
Peter Sault
Ivy Poison

See: **Bernstein, Xavier**

naivetè, nigh-eev-TAY or nigh-EEV-uh-**TAY** or
naïvetè NAH-eev-**TAY**

*Two little old ladies bought used Volkswagen
Beetles. One of them said, "I just looked under
the hood, and I don't have an engine." The other
one said, "Well, don't worry. I just opened my
trunk and there's an extra one in there."*

naphtha NAF-thuh
Avoid: NAP-thuh
Definition: a colorless, volatile petroleum product
See: **diphtheria, diphthong, ophthalmologist**

nausea NAW-zee-uh, NAW-shuh or NAW-zhuh

nauseous NAW-shus, NAW-zee-us or NAW-see-us
Don't say you're *nauseous* when you're only
nauseated.

Neandertal nee-**AN**-dur-TAWL
Don't say: nee-**AN**-druh-THAWL

nèe, nee nay
Don't say: nee

Nevada nuh-VA-duh
Don't say: nuh-VAY-duh

Newfoundland **NOO**-fund-LUND or **NOO**-fund-LAND
Avoid: noo-FOUND-land

New Haven noo HAY-v 'n
Don't say: NOO hay-v'n

New Haven is stressed on the middle syllable, just
like the Connecticut towns of New London, New
Britain, New Milford, New Preston, New Hartford
and New Canaan, and such other places as New
Hampshire, New England, New Jersey, New Bruns-
wick, New Guinea, New Zealand and New Delhi.

New Orleans noo OR-linz
noo OR-lee-inz
NOO or-LEENZ
See: **LaJolla**

WOTSA MATTA, JOE?

I GOTTA NICHE!

RLS

niche nich (rhymes with *itch*)
Never say: nish or neesh!
Niche doesn't rhyme with *quiche*.

It does rhyme with *stitch*.

A subway inspector named Stein (that's styn, rhyming with wine) was checking the tracks one day when an unscheduled train suddenly rounded a curve and careened toward him. He sought frantically for a recess in the wall, found one and scrambled into it. And so it was that a niche in time saved Stein.

See: **cache** and **crèche**

nihilism NY-i-LIZ-'m
Don't say" NEE-i-LIZ-'m

nolo contendere NOH-loh kuhn-TEN-duh-ree
Definition: a plea of no contest to a criminal charge

no question but There's no question this phrase is a double negative. If you said, "There's no question <u>but</u> this phrase is a double negative," you'd be saying there is a question even though you probably meant that it's unquestionable.

nonpareil NON-puh-**REL**
Don't say: NON-puh-**REEL**
Definition: peerless, having no equal

Northampton north-HAMP-t'n or north-AMP-t'n
(Massachusetts) A professor from Northampton who often wrote to me years ago told me that this city is properly pronounced north-AMP-t'n, as in England. My father and Phil's grandfather, Hampton Lee Steele, always kept his *h*, whether asked, "Are you going south, Hampton?" or "Are you going north, Hampton?"

Norwich NOR-ich (in Norwich, Connecticut and
(Connecticut) Norwich, England)
NOR-wich (for those not from either Norwich)

nth You can stump almost anyone by asking them to try to think of a three-letter word without a vowel. You can stump them to the nth degree. By the way, it's better not to use *them* when your antecedent is singular—here it's *anyone*—but unless you can rewrite your sentence to avoid the issue, *them* sometimes sounds better than using *him or her* a lot. It's now rather common, and, we think, acceptable, at least in speech, to use *they*, *them* or *their*, instead of *he*, *him* or *his*, after a singular antecedent such as *one* or *anyone* in order to avoid excluding half the human race.

nuclear NOO-klee-ur
Never say: NOO-kyuh-lur or NOO-kyoo-lur

nuptial NUHP-sh'l (tial as in *partial* and *martial*)
Watch out for: NUHP-shoo-'l and NUP-choo-'l
See: **controversial**

The preacher had just united two hippies in holy wedlock. He looked at them in puzzlement and then asked, "Will one of you please kiss the bride?"

octogenarian AHK-tuh-juh-**NAIR**-ee-'n
An eighty-year old lady invited some friends to her birthday party. "Are you going to have candles on the birthday cake? one asked. The octogenarian replied, "This is to be a birthday party, not a torchlight procession."

often AWF-'n
Don't say: AWF-t'n
The *t* in *often* and *soften* is silent.

Ojai OH-high
(California) Don't say: OH-jay

Omaha OH-muh-HAW (rhymes with *Wichita* and *Utah*)
(Nebraska)

omnivorous ahm-NIV-ur-us
Don't say: AHM-nee-**VOR**-us

ophthalmologist AHF-thahl-**MAHL**-uh-jist
Watch out for: AHP-thuh-**MAHL**-uh-jist
See: **diphtheria, diphthong, naphtha**

When the eye doctor finished examining the patient, he had to report that the man had double-vision. The patient became angry and jumped down from the chair exclaiming, "Double vision, my foot! You are both idiots."

Oregon OR-uh-gun
Don't say: OR-uh-**GAHN**

orgy, orgiastic OR-jee, OR-jee-**AS**-tik

Don't say: OR-gee, OR-gee-**AS**-tik

I first interviewed Ted at the end of the '42 season. The Sporting News reported: "Williams was interviewed by Steele over WTIC on his sports show. Ted revealed...the cause for his drop in batting average this year — if you can call Ted's .356 a drop. (Last year he hit .406.)Ted said the ball used this season appeared less lively, the playing fields were not always in the best condition, thus preventing many ground balls from going as possible hits and that many games were played under conditions which under normal times would result in postponement, but were played because the teams were not sure the season could be finished, in view of the war." These are stills of TV footage from "Close-Up on Sports" on Channel 3 after Ted finished his Hall of Fame career.

orthodontist OR-thoh-**DAHN**-tist

Pakistan During the early 1930s in England delegates and students from British India began planning the independence of their homelands. The Muslims among them proposed a separate nation and suggested that it be called *Pakistan*, an acronym for the regions that would make it up, and a particularly apt choice for many who saw *Pakistan* also as Hindi and/or Persian for "land of the pure." But there is some difference of opinion about which regions make up the acronym. All agree that P is for Punjab and K is for Kashmir. Some say S is for Sindh and TAN is for Baluchistan. Some say A is for Aghania while others say it is for Assam. Another view is that three of the letters stand for three Muslim homelands of Asia not a part of Pakistan but with which it might one day be united: Iran, Tukharistan and Afghanistan.

palindrome Words, phrases or sentences that read the same backwards:

Able was I ere I saw Elba
A man, a plan, a canal, Panama
if I had a hifi

palm pahm
Don't say: pahlm
One syllable only; the *l* is silent. See: **alms, balm, caulk, calm, caulk, psalm** and **qualm**

pantomime **PAN**-toh-**MIGHM** (mime rhymes with *dime*)
Don't say: **PAN**-toh-**MIGHN** (Don't rhyme it with *dine*.) *Mime* has two *m*'s and no *n*.

papal PAY-p'l
Don't say: PAP-'l

paradigm PAIR-uh-dim or PAIR-uh-dighm
(dighm sounds like *dime*)
Definition: model or example

paraphernalia PAIR-uh-fur-**NAIL**-yuh
Don't say: PAIR-uh-fuh-**NAIL**-yuh or
PAIR-uh-fur-**NAIL**-ee-uh

parliamentary PAHR-luh-**MEN**-tuh-ree
Don't say: PAR-luh-men-**TAIR**-ee

pastoral PAS-tur-'l
Don't say: pa-STOR-'l
See **electoral** and **mayoral**

A Labor Department investigator checked on a farmer who reportedly was paying his help below-standard wages. The farmer willingly introduced him to the hired hands. "This here is Gordon. He milks the cows, works in the fields and gets ninety-five dollars a week. And this young lady is Betsy Lou. She cooks and cleans and gets seventy-five dollars a week, plus room and board."

"Sounds okay so far," said the inspector. "Is there anyone else?"

"Only the half-wit," replied the farmer. "He gets twenty dollars a week, tobacco, and room and board."

"I'd like to meet him."

"You're talkin' to him right now," the farmer crisply pointed out.

pathos   PAY-thahs (rhymes with *MS-DOS* and *Haas*,
         as in golfer *Jay Haas*)
         Don't say: PATH-aws or PATH-ohs
         See: **ethos, bathos, Eros** and **kudos**

patina   PAT-ih-nuh or PAT'n-uh
         Don't say: puh-TEE-nuh

patronize   PAY-truh-nyz or PA-truh-nyz

Pawtucket   p'-TUHK-it
(Rhode Island)   Out-of-towners say paw-TUHK-it

pejorative   p'-JOR-uh-tiv
         Never accent the first syllable.

penal, penalize   PEE-nul, PEE-nuh-lyz
         Not as good: PEN-uh-lyz

         In Cincinnati's Court of Common Pleas, a convicted
         housebreaker greeted his penal fate with exhilarated
         expectation—until the court clerk hastened to
         correct the judge who had just sentenced him to
         five years in the Ohio State University.

Four generations of Steeles. I became a proud great grand-father, Robert a proud grandfather and his son Jeff a proud father when Alexander Edward Steele was born in 2000.

pendulum PEN-joo-lum or PEN-dyoo-lum
Avoid: PEN-duh-lum

peninsular puh-NIN-syoo-lahr or puh-NIN-suh-lahr

penitentiary PEN-ih-**TEN**-shur-ee (rhymes with *century*)
Don't say: PEN-ih-**TEN**-shee-ar-ee

In 1942 the Connecticut sports writers' association held its annual sports banquet at the state prison in Wethersfield. My job as toastmaster drew this comment from The Monthly Record: "Bob pulled the stunt that stole the show. With a grand build-up which went something like this–"It is my privilege and pleasure to now introduce to you a world famous man, an industrial giant, a globe trotter who has been to every corner of the world, a man whose name is on the tip of the tongue of every American — none other than Henry Ford.' Well, the house went wild. Almost to a man they stood, handclapping and cheering. This continued for a full minute, but no Henry Ford. Bob glanced anxiously right and left. His face expressed great consternation. Bob finally explained that he thought that Henry was in the crowd as he had seen his car parked outside. Did ears burn! Sheepishly we sat down. What a shame this guy Steele is a successful commentator. What a swell con-man he would have made."

pentathlon   pen-TATH-lahn
Don't say: pen-TATH-uh-lahn. Three syllables!
See: **biathlon, triathlon** and **decathlon**

peripheral   puh-RIF-ur-'l
Don't say: fuh-RIF-ur-'l

perplexing plurals

We'll begin with the fox
And the plural is foxes.
But the plural of ox
Should never be oxes.
One fowl is a goose.
The plural is geese.
But the plural of moose
Won't therefore be meese
So also for mouse,
The plural is mice.
But for house
It's houses.
We never say hice.
And since plural of man
Is always called men,
For the plural of pan
Why can't we say pen?
The one may be that
And three may be those.
Yet rat in the plural
Is never called rose.
And the masculine pronouns
Are he, his and him
But imagine the feminine
She, shis and shim.
So English I fancy
You all will agree
Is the most lawless language
You ever did see.

AUTHOR UNKNOWN

percolator PUR-kuh-LAY-t'r
Don't say: **PURK**-yoo-LAY-t'r

persona pur-SOH-nuh
Don't say: pur-SAH-nuh
The plural is *personae* (pur-SOH-nee) or *personas*.

pianist pee-AN-ist
British: PEE-an-ist

picture PIK-chur
Watch out for: PICH-ur

Pierre peer
(South Dakota) Don't say: pee-AIR

pinochle, **PEE**-NUHK-'l
pinocle Don't say: PEE-nah-k'l

piquant PEE-kint
Also: pee-KANT or pee-KAHNT
Definition: pleasantly spicy or pungent

placard PLAK-urd
Don't say: pla-KARD

placate PLAY-kayt or PLAK-ayt (sounds like *plaque ate*)
Don't say: play-KAYT

plaintain PLAN-t'n
Don't say: plan-TAYN

plebeian pluh-BEE-in
Don't say: PLEE-bee-in

poinsettia poyn-SET-ee-uh
Never say: poyn-SET-uh
A teacher asked her class, "If the poinsettia plant

reminds us of Christmas, what plant reminds you of Easter?" A little girl eagerly replied, "An egg plant."

Porsche　porsh
Avoid: POR-shuh

Portuguese　**POR**-tyoo-GEES or **POR**-tyoo-GEEZ
See: **Chinese** and **Japanese**

posthumous　PAHS-chuh-mus
Don't say: post-HYOO-mus

Even though *posthumous* looks like *post-humous*, it's not pronounced that way. During the Middle Ages, an *h* was added to the Latin word *postumus*, probably because its meaning then, as now, involved the idea of "after death" and so suggested humus, a Latin word for earth or ground. The *h* did not change the pronunciation.

The guy who keeps telling you you can't take it with you is planning on taking it with him.

Rocky Marciano, heavy-weight champion of the world, was the only undefeated boxing champion in any weight class. Between 1947 and 1955, he won a record 49 straight fights, 43 by knockout.

Poughkeepsie　puh-KIP-see
(New York)　Don't say: puh-KEEP-see

Powell,
R. Baden- Robert Baden-Powell (1857-1941), the founder of the world scout movement, including the Boy Scouts, being English, pronounced his name BAYD-'n-POH-'l, not POW-'l.

pretty PRIH-tee
Don't say: PREH-tee

preferable PREF-ur-uh-b'l
Don't say: pre-FUR-uh-b'l

prelude PREL-yood
Don't say: PRAY-lood

premises PREM-ih-siz
Don't say: PREM-ih-seez

premonition PREE-muh-**NISH**-in
Don't say: PREM-uh-**NISH**-in

pre-nuptial See: nuptial

preparatory prih-**PAIR**-uh-TOR-ee
Don't say: **PREP**-ur-uh-TOR-ee or **PREP**-uh-ruh-TOR-ee

prepositions Generally avoid ending sentences with a preposition, but feel free to avoid this rule if the alternative seems unnatural. As the great authority on English usage, Henry W. Fowler, wrote, "The power of saying...*People worth talking to* instead of *People with whom it is worthwhile to talk,* is not one to be lightly surrendered."

prerogative prih-**RAHG**-uh-tiv or pruh-**RAHG**-uh-tiv
Avoid: pree-RAHG-uh-tiv
And pur-RAHG-uh-tiv is not your prerogative.

presentation   PREZ-in-**TAY**-shin
Also: PREE-zen-**TAY**-shin

Nurse says to the patient, "Can't you try to smile and look happy for the doctor when he comes in?" The guy says, "I'm not gonna smile. I feel miserable." "Well couldn't you manage a little smile for the doctor's benefit? He's so worried about your case."

president   PREZ-uh-dint
Watch out for PREZ-dint and even PREZ-n'nt

A mother hearing her little boy say "hellava" scolded him, "Young man, I don't want you to use that kind of language." "But George Bush says it," he protested. The mother responded, "Then don't play with him."

Presley   PRES-lee
(Elvis)   Don't say: PREZ-lee

prestigious   preh-STIJ-us
Also: preh-STEEJ-us
Don't say: preh-STIJ-ee-us

prima (ballerina)   PREE-muh (ballerina) and PREE-muh (donna)
and   The Latin/Italian pronunciation survives in these
prima (donna)   phrases if not in *prima facie*.

prima facie   PRY-muh FAY-shee or PRY-muh FAY-shuh
These anglicized pronunciations are too entrenched to complain about, and the Latin pronunciation, PREE-muh- FA-chee-ay (FA as in *fatuous*) is rarely heard. Avoid going halfway, partly Latin and partly anglicized, as in PREE-muh FAY-shuh. If you like PREE-muh give *facie* a Latin pronunciation as well.

primer PRY-mur
(paint) Don't confuse with the same word (different pronunciation) meaning an introductory or basic textbook such as *The New England Primer*.

primer PRIM-ur
(textbook) Don't confuse with the same word (different pronunciation) for a preliminary coat of paint.

proboscis proh-BAHS-is
Don't say: pruh-BAHS-kis

process PROH-ses or PRAH-ses
The plural is PROH-ses-iz, not PROH-seh-seez. Don't be fooled by words like **crisis, basis** and **thesis**. The plural of crisis is *crises,* pronounced KRIGH-seez.

promulgate **PRAHM**-ul-GAYT
Don't say: **PRAHM**-yool-GAYT

pronunciation This word is sometimes pronounced, and even spelled, as if it were *pronounciation*.

prophesied PRAHF-uh-**SYD**
Don't say: PRAHF-uh-**SEED**
The verb *prophesy* is pronounced PRAHF-uh-**SIGH,** while the noun *prophecy* is pronounced PRAHF-uh-SEE.

proscribe Don't confuse *proscribe* (to condemn or prohibit) with *prescribe* (to set down a rule or course to be followed).

protein PROH-teen
Don't say: PROH-tee-in

provost   PROH-vohst
Also: PRAHV-uhst

psalm   sahm
Don't say: sahlm
One syllable only; the *l* is silent. See: **alms, balm, caulk, calm, caulk, palm** and **qualm**

Pulitzer   PUL-it-sur (sounds like *pull it sir*)
Also: PYOO-lit-sur

Joseph Pulitzer (1847-1911), the Hungarian-born American journalist and publisher, was a founder of the Columbia School of Journalism and the Pulitzer Prizes.

pulpit   PUL-pit (pul sounds like *pull*, rhymes with *bull*).
Don't say: PUL-pit (PUL as in *gull* and *lull*)
Think of the pull of the pulpit, never a lull.

qualm kwahm
The *l* is silent. See: **balk, balm, calm** and **caulk**

quasi, quasi- KWAY-zigh, KWAH-zee
Also: KWAY-sigh, KWAH-see
See: **anti-, semi-, multi-**

quay kee
Avoid: kay

query KWEER-ee or KWAIR-ee

quintuplet kwin-TUHP-lit or kwin-TOO-plit

Quito KEE-toh
(Ecuador) Don't say: KWEE-toh

quixotic kwik-SAHT-ik
Don't say: kwig-ZAHT-ik or kee-HOH-tik

Racicot (Mark)   RAH-skoh (sounds like *Roscoe*)
A former governor of Montana, Mr. Racicot
became head of the Republican National
Committee in 2001.

raconteur   RAK-ohn-**TUR**
Never say: RAK-ohn-**TOOR**
See: **connoisseur, entrepreneur** and other words
from the French ending in *eur*: **saboteur, auteur,
amateur, chauffeur, provocateur, restaurateur,
hauteur, liqueur, de rigeur, voyeur**

ragg mopp   "Rag Mop" was written in 1909 by Helen S.
Eaton. Some lyrics!

> M
> I say M-O
> M-O-P
> M-O-P-P
> Mop
> M-O-P-P
> Mop Mop Mop Mop
> R
> I say R-A
> R-A-G
> R-A-G-G
> Rag
> R-A-G-G M-O-P-P
> Rag Mop

Is it any wonder the song became a favorite on
both *The Bob Steele Show* and *Sesame Street*?

ragout	ra-GOO (ra as in *rag*)
	Don't say: ra-GOOT
Rainier (Mount)	ray-NEER
Rainier (Prince)	reh-NYAY
Raleigh (North Carolina)	RAW-lee Don't say: RAHL-ee
rampart, **ramparts**	RAM-part(s) Don't say: ram-PART(S) or RAMP-urt(s)

José, a Mexican boy, saved all his money so he could come to the U.S.A. and see a World Series game. José arrived in New York (of course—not Boston) and went to the ticket booth. The man told him, "I'm sorry, kid, but we are sold out for the Series."

"But I have come all the way from Mexico to see a game," pleaded José.

"Ah, go climb a flag pole," quipped the ticket man.

When José arrived home in Mexico, he told his pal, Pedro, what had happened, and Pedro asked, "So, did you see the game?"

"Si," said José, "I did what the man said and climbed the flag pole in Yankee Stadium. Oh, but everybody was so nice. They all stood up and looked at me and with a band assisting them, they sang up to me, 'José, can you see?' "

rapine   RAP-in
Don't say: RAY-pyn or RAY-peen
Definition: violent theft, plunder

RBI, RBI's, RBIs   Ted Williams led the American League in Runs Batted In four times, Babe Ruth five times and Lou Gehrig an amazing eight times. One run batted in is abbreviated RBI. How should two runs batted in be designated? 2 RBI, 2 RBI's or 2 RBIs? The question is not as easy as 1 mph versus 100 mph.

We hear "RBI" so frequently in the world of sports that it has arguably reached a status beyond an abbreviation, a unit in itself, making it as natural to say 2 RBIs as to say 2 hits. But many insist that since it's "runs batted in" that's meant, the pluralizing s just doesn't belong at the end. And should those who put the s at the end also use an apostrophe, or leave it out: RBI's or RBIs? See: 's.

Of course, the abbreviation is sometimes written in lower case, and 2 rbis is a stretch. Even those who prefer RBI's or RBIs probably would not add an s when using the expression as an adjective. The RBI leader, not the RBI's or RBIs leader, even though what's meant is the Runs Batted In leader, not the Run Batted In leader.

RBI for the plural is preferred by sportswriters, probably resulting from their somewhat more formal medium with its greater time for reflection and bias toward consistent and reasoned standards. Sportscasters are less consistent, resulting no doubt from the lesser formality of speech and the natural tendency of speech toward inflection in order to clarify distinctions. Very informally, "ribbies" is sometimes used as well.

We don't know whether it's something about baseball that encourages this kind of concern and speculation on our part. It may just be a family birth defect.

In digital graphics, professionals who start with one dpi (dot per inch) have to choose between 2 dpi and 2 dpi's for two dots per inch and usually go with 2 dpi.

The possessive *'s* can pose the same problem as the plural *'s*. Probably no one would hesitate to say the FBI's witness, or the Federal Bureau of Investigation's witness, surely passing up the Federal Bureau's of Investigation witness, even though it is the Bureau's witness.

realty   REE-'l-tee
Never say: REE-luh-tee
The *a* in *realty* comes before the *l*, not between the *l* and the *t*.

The same is true for *realtor*: REE-'l-tur. Some dictionaries give only *Realtor* (capitalized). The word was trademarked by the National Association of Real Estate Boards, and dictionaries specifically define a realtor/Realtor as a member of that association. Technically, the word should not only be capitalized but followed by the symbol ®. One can understand the proprietary interests of Kleenex, Xerox and other products that have become commonly used words, but the resistance of commercial interests to *kleenex, xerox, realty* and similar words seems excessive, if not counter-productive.

reason is because

Grammatically wrong. *Because* shouldn't be used to introduce a noun clause. The *because* is redundant. Think of it as a double positive. Instead, say the *reason is that.*

One fella says, "My wife lost her credit card but we haven't reported it." The other fella asks, "Why not?" The first fella answers, "Well, the reason is that the guy who found it is spending less than she was."

Notice the first fella didn't say, "Well, the reason is because..."

recuperate ree-**KOO**-puh-RAYT or ree-**KYOO**-puh-RAYT

relief still spelled r-e-l-i-e-f

relinquish rih-LING-kwish
Not as good: rih-LINK-wish
See: delinquent

remonstrate rih-MAHN-strayt
Don't say: **REM**-uhn-STRAYT

Cop: "What are you doing on the streets at this hour?"
Drunk: "I'm going to a lecture.
Cop: You won't find any lectures around here at 3 a.m."
Drunk: "Wanna bet? Just follow me home!"

repartee REP-ur-**TEE** or REP-ahr-**TEE**
Don't say: REP-ahr-TAY

repeat again You can repeat something again, but only if you've already repeated it once.

repercussion REE-pur-**KUHSH**-in
Don't say: REP-ur-**KUHSH**-in
And don't make the *cussion* sound like *cushion*.

reprise rih-PREEZ
Don't say: rih-PRYZ

reservoir **REZ**-ur-VWAHR
Not as good: **REZ**-ur-VWAWR
The *voir* should rhyme with *far*, not *war*.

respite REHS-pit
Don't say: RE-spight or REE-spight

restaurateur RES-tur-uh-**TUR**
Never say: RES-tur-uh-**TOOR**

The only thing worse than RES-tur-uh-**TOOR** is RES-tur-ahn-**TOOR**. So rarely do people even notice that *restaurateur* has no *n* in it, that you can probably take advantage of their ignorance with a wager—perhaps one for a meal at your favorite restaurant. A restaurateur is one who restores. His or her place of business is a restaurant.

A lady from Springfield says, "The average waiter walks 12 miles a day. No wonder my soup is always cold when I get it."

At the Hartford Club, in 1957, I asked Bob Hope how the course looked to him. "I'll let you know," he answered. "If it plays well, I may buy it."

Reverend Reverend, like Honorable, is properly used only as an adjective, and only with the full name or the initials and the last name of the person to whom it refers: The Reverend Thomas Elliott, or The Reverend T. S. Elliott. It should not be used in the same way as Professor or Doctor before a surname. Thus, Doctor Elliott or Dr. Elliott, but not Reverend Elliott or Rev. Elliott, and not by itself, as in "Hello, Reverend." These rules, of course, are frequently disregarded.

ribald RIB-'ld
Don't say: RIGH-b'ld or RIGH-bald (RIGH sounds like *rye*.)

ridiculous rih-DIK-yuh-luhs
Don't say: rih-DIK-yoo-luhs

rigmarole **RIG**-muh-ROHL
Don't say: **RIG**-uh-muh-ROHL

The variant spelling, *rigamarole*, however, may be so pronounced.

romance roh-MANS
Also, as a noun: ROH-mans

Roosevelt ROH-zuh-velt
Don't say: ROOZ-uh-velt

Everybody called TR ROOZ-uh-velt. By the 1930s, however, with the influence of radio, people learned to call FDR ROH-zuh-velt.

roseate ROH-zee-it
Definition: rosy, highly optimistic

rotund roh-TUHND
Don't say: ROH-tund

ruse Rooz
Don't say: roos

Conversation overheard in a beauty parlor in West Hartford.
Hairdresser: "Shall I give you a shampoo, Madam?"
Mrs. Gotrocks: "I can afford the best—you'll give me a genuine poo or nothing at all!"

's There are no clear, simple rules that tell you whether to add an *'s* to indicate the possessive form for words ending in *s* or *z*. Most would write, and say, *Julius's horse* rather than *Julius' horse*, but few would write or say *for righteousness's sake* or *Ulysses's wife*. Plural possessives ending in *s* take only an apostrophe—not *'s*: *their fathers' land* or *The Hundred Years' War*. As well as indicating the possessive, *'s* is commonly used to indicate the plural of a figure, a letter of the alphabet and a word referred to as a word: the 1990's, two b's and second of the two word's. Sometimes the apostrophe can be spared: 1990s, but that's not always practical; just try to write "dot your i's and cross your t's" without the apostrophe, or even "dot your j's and cross your f's.". See: **RBI**

sabotage **SA**-boh-TAHZH
Don't say: SA-boh-TAJ
See: **garage, corsage, espionage, massage, montage**

saboteur SA-boh-**TUR**
Never say: SA-boh-**TOOR**
See: **connoisseur, entrepreneur** and other words from the French ending in *eur*: **auteur, raconteur, chauffeur, provocateur, restaurateur, hauteur, liqueur, de rigeur, voyeur**

sacrilegious SAC-rih-**LIJ**-us
Try writing this word a few times to get used to the spelling. It's not *sac-religious*. The *e* and the

first *i* of *religious* are reversed in *sacrilegious*, even though it sounds like *sac-religious*.

An Essex yachtsman, who had just been initiated into the mysteries of the art of navigation, suddenly put aside his sextant and shouted to his companion, "Take off your hat."

"Why should I?" asked his bewildered friend.

"Because according to my calculations," replied the yachtsman, "we are in the center of St. Patrick's Cathedral."

sacrosanct **SAK**-roh-SAYNKT

Salina (Kansas) suh-LIGH-nuh (LIGH sounds like *lie*.)

Salinas (California) suh-LEE-nuhs

Salisbury (Connecticut) SAWLZ-bair-ee
Salisbury steak is pronounced like the town in Connecticut, but some towns by this name throughout the world may be pronounced SAWLZ-buh-ree.

salmon SAM-un
Don't say: SAL-mun
See: **alms, balk, balm, calm, caulk, qualm**
And the first *l* in *salmonella* is likewise silent.

Didn't Sal Monella play shortstop for the Yankees?

sandwich SAND-which
But it is hard to be fussy about a word like *sandwich*, so we see no great ham–or harm, in SAN-which.

A man was arrested in a sandwich shop—charged with assault with intent to pepper.

San Francisco   SAN fran-**SIS**-koh
Don't say: SAN frun-**SIS**-koh

*A fellow went to check-in at Bradley Airport.
"Your plane goes to San Francisco in ten minutes,"
he was told. "Boy, that's moving," he replied.*

Saturday   See: -day

savant   suh-VAHNT
Don't say: sa-VOHNT

scallop   SKAH-lup or SKAL-up

schism   skizm or sizm

scion   SY-un
Don't say: SKY-un

A scion of Connecticut's famous Charter Oak is
one of the most notable of the many great trees in
Hartford's Bushnell Park.

scourge   skurj (rhymes with *urge*)
Don't say: skoorj

secretary   **SEK**-rih-TAIR-ee
Don't say: **SEK**-ur-TAIR-ee
Connecticut and many states have a Secretary of
the State, not a Secretary of State.

*My wife doesn't care how good looking my
secretary is—as long as he's efficient.*

secretive   SEE-krih-tiv
Also: see-KREE-tiv. *Secreted*, however, should only
be pronounced sih-KREE-tid

The boss called one of his employees into the
office. "Jones," he said, "I've been watching you.
You get in early and leave late. You've never

missed a day. You get all your work done and help Smith when he's overloaded; you've never complained and never asked for a raise. Tell me, just what the hell are you up to?"

sedentary SED-'n-TAIR-ee

Don't say: suh-DEN-tuh-ree

Plumber: "I understand you have something here that doesn't work."
Housewife: "Yes, he's in the living room on the couch."

Interviewing Wilbur Shaw, three-time winner of the Indianapolis 500 (1937, 1939 and 1940) who became the President of the Indianapolis Speedway.

semi- SEM-ee

Don't say: SEM-igh (*igh* sounds like *eye*)
See: **anti-, multi-** and **quasi-**

seminal SEM-ih-n'l

Don't say: SEE-mih-n'l

senile SEE-nyl (nyl sounds like *Nile*).

Don't say: SEN-yl (yl sounds like *I'll*)

You are getting old if it takes you longer to rest than it did to get tired.

sentence   SEN-tints
Watch out for SEN-ints. Don't forget the *t*.

serpentine   SUR-pin-teen or SUR-pin-tighn

servile   SUR-v'l
British: SUR-vyl (*vyl* sounds like *vile*)

See: **docile, fertile, fragile, futile, hostile, mobile**

settee   se-TEE

sheik, sheikh   sheek or shayk (for either spelling)

sherbet   SHUR-bit
Don't say SHUR-burt

sheriff   Watch the spelling! Just one *r*. Anybody who spells it with two *r*'s deserves to be plugged!

short-lived short-LYVD (rhymes with *thrived* and *arrived*)
British: short-LIVD (as in *outlived*).

siege seej
Don't say: seezh

Sigourney The street in Hartford is SI-gur-nee.
The actress is sih-GOR-nee.

simultaneity SIGH-mul-tuh-**NEE**-ih-tee
Don't say: SIGH-mul-tuh-**NAY**-ih-tee
See: **deity, heterogeneity, homogeneity, spontaneity**

sinecure **SIGH**-nuh-KYOOR or **SIN**-uh-KYOOR
Definition: a position that brings advantage with little responsibility

Sinn Fein shin FAYN

siren SIGH-ren
Don't say: SIGH-reen

sobriquet SO-bruh-**KET**, SO-bruh-**KAY**, **SO**-bruh-KET, **SO**-bruh-KET
Definition: a nickname

Socrates SAH-kruh-teez

Years ago I was kidding around about Plato's teacher "SO-krayts" and quickly got a call from a concerned listener. So, back on the air, I brought up the learned caller complaining about "SO-krayts." After I mentioned orange crates and grapefruit crates, I got no further complaints.

solecism SAHL-uh-siz'm
Don't say: SOHL-uh-siz'm

sonorous SAH-nur-us or suh-NOR-us
Don't say: SOH-nur-us or soh-NOR-us

sophomore SAHF-uh-MOR
Also: SAHF-mor
Never say: SOWTH-mor (like *south more*)

"I hear you have a boy in college. Is he going to become a doctor, an engineer, or a lawyer, perhaps?" The slow, quizzical answer was: "Right now the big question is: Is he going to become a sophomore?"

Spanish names English speakers are unavoidably inconsistent when it comes to pronouncing Spanish names. Red Sox fans have had no problem with Pedro Martinez (mahr-TEEN-es), but for Latinos of less renown the name is usually anglicized to mahr-TEEN-ez, and even Pedro's teammate, Manny Ramirez, is usually pronounced with a *z* rather than *s*. Chavez is often anglicized to CHA-vez, or worse, SHA-vez, or even shuh-VEZ, and Jimenez to hee-MAYN-ez, or worse, JIH-mih-nez. Better to say CHA-ves and hee-MAYN-es.

specialty SPESH-ul-tee
Don't confuse with the word the British prefer: *speciality* (SPESH-ee-**AL**-ih-tee).

species SPEE-sheez
Don't say: SPEE-seez

Spokane spoh-KAN
(Washington) Don't say: spoh-KAYN

spontaneity SPAHN-tuh-**NEE**-ih-tee
Not as good: SPAHN-tuh-**NAY**-ih-tee
See: **deity, heterogeneity, homogeneity, simultaneity**

spoonerism   An unintentional interchange of sounds in two words, usually the initial sounds, with humorous effect—now so well known that it's no longer capitalized.

An Oxford dean, William A. Spooner (1844-1930) intending to say, "May I show you to another seat?" is reputed to have said instead, "May I sew you to another sheet?"

Other popular attributions to Dr. Spooner are:
a well-boiled icicle
a blushing crow
a half-warmed fish
our shoving leopard
our queer old Dean
You hissed my mystery lectures.
My boy, it's kisstomary to cuss the bride.
Take this in aid of Oxford's beery wenches.
When the boys come home from France, we'll have hags flung out.
Pardon me, madam, you are occupewing my pie.

The *Oxford Dictionary of Quotations*, 3rd edition (1979), gives only one spoonerism ("weight of rages"), and says: "Many other Spoonerisms, such as those given in the previous editions of O.D.Q., are now known to be apocryphal." The Oxford English Dictionary says the word *spoonerism* was "known in colloquial use in Oxford from about 1885." In his diary entry of May 9, 1904, Spooner wrote that someone he met at dinner "seemed to think he owed me some gratitude for the many 'Spoonerisms' which I suppose have appeared in Tit Bits." One of the undergraduates who attested "weight of rages" commented: "Well, I've been up for four years, and never heard the Spoo make a Spoonerism before, and now he makes a damned rotten one at the last minute."

spurious SPYOOR-ee-us
Don't say: SPUR-ee-us

stationary, **STAY**-shu-NAIR-ee
stationery Don't say: STAY-shun-ree

You can remember the distinction between these two words by noting that the one spelled with an *e* is the one that relates to envelopes.

An Old Lyme customer asked a stationer's clerk to advise him on the selection of a greeting card. "I want to send a card to a man who is drilling for water on my property," the man said, "but I've been unable to find an appropriate card. What would you suggest?"

"I think you ought to send him a 'get well' card," the clerk replied.

statistics stuh-TIHS-tiks
Don't say: suh-TIHS-tiks

I was amazed to learn that a man is run over every 18 minutes in Los Angeles. Poor fellow!

Sugar Ray Leonard successfully defended his welterweight title in New Haven and I was the ring announcer. Sugar Ray's career spanned over 20 years, his last fight coming in 1997. There's no question that he was one of the all-time great fighters.

status STAT-us
British: STAY-tus

strength strengkth
Don't say: strenth
See: **length**

stomach STUM-uk (rhymes with *hammock*, *havoc* and *Potomac*). Don't say: STUM-ik

subsidiary suhb-**SID**-ee-AIR-ee
Don't say: suhb-SID-ur-ee or suhb-**SID**-ur-AIR-ee

succinct suhk-SINGKT
Do not say: suh-SINGKT

Sunday See: **-day**

superfluous soo-PUR-floo-us
Don't say: soo-PUR-fil-us or SOO-pur-**FLOO**-us

supposed suh-POHZD
Don't say: suh-POH-zid
The *ed* ending is heard in full in *supposedly* but not in *supposed*. See: **alleged** and **marked**

surprise sur-PRYZ
Watch out for suh-PRYZ

The difference is very slight but still worth keeping in mind. Other words in which the *r* tends to be dropped are *quarter*, *February* and *library*. Another consonant that's sometimes dropped is *t*, as in *quantity* (quan'ity) and *bankruptcy*.

sycophant SIK-uh-funt
Don't say: SIK-oh-fant
Definition: a self-serving flatterer

Syracuse SEER-uh-kyoos
(New York) Don't say: SEER-uh-kyooz

syringe suh-RINJ
Also: SEER-inj

syrup SEER-up or SUR-up

Szwlnfhewskmczy On the Associated Press sports wire, June 5, 1948: "Miss Hart was beaten by a Hungarian competitor, Mrs. Szwlnfhewskmczy. Scores were 4-6, 6-3, 6-3. While an upset, the loss was not too surprising as Miss Hart has not been feeling well for several days."

Radio announcers, having come upon this item cold, also felt ill for several days, it is reported.

tacit,   TAS-it, TAS-ih-turn
taciturn   Don't say: TAK-it, TAK-ih-turn

Tangier   This town in Morocco near the Strait of Gibraltar is not *Tangiers*. Don't confuse it with Algiers, Algeria.

temperamental   **TEM**-pruh-MEN-t'l or **TEM**-pur-uh-MEN-t'l
Avoid: **TEM**-pur-MEN-t'l

temperature   TEM-pur-uh-chur or TEM-pruh-chur
Don't say: TEM-pur-chur

textile   TEKS-tyl or TEKS-t'l
See: **fertile, fragile, futile, hostile, juvenile, mobile, servile** and **versatile. Textile, juvenile** and **domicile,** however, have bucked the trend of these words pronounced with a short *i* and are often pronounced with a long *i* as in Britain.

Thames (River)   thayms (in Connecticut), tems (in England)
Americans may have adopted *thayms* even without the advocacy of Noah Webster, but the lexicographer's ubiquitous spelling book was a powerful influence encouraging Americans to do what they were already inclined to do, pronouncing English names and other words the way they were spelled and to spell them the way they sound. Thus English words ending in *our* such as *labour* and *honour* lost the *u*. But Webster's insistence on

pronouncing Greenwich GREEN-wich instead of
GREN-ich may have lost out to a fondness for
what sounded British and hence upper class.
Webster also was unsuccessful in battling WU-stur
for Worcester. Other American pronunciations of
places with Old World names needed no help from
Webster. See: **Berlin, Coventry, Glastonbury,
Norwich, Salisbury**

theater, theatre THEE-tur or THEE-uh-tur (for either spelling)

these, *These* and *those* are plural, *kind* is singular.
those kind Say *"this kind"* or *"these kinds,"* and *"that kind"*
or *"those kinds."*

Thursday See: -day

timbre TIM-bur or TAM-bur

tomato tuh-MAY-toh or tuh-MAH-toh
Add *es* for the plural: *tomatoes*. Likewise for
potato, but for *buffalo* and *mosquito*, take your
choice, *buffalos* or *buffaloes, mosquitos* or *mos-
quitoes*. It's not hard to understand why we're
more flexible about animal life than plant life.
Offending a vegetable is not nearly as dangerous.

toot tut (rhymes with *foot*) or toot (rhymes with
boot) in the Al Jolson song "Toot, Toot, Tootsie,
Good-bye."

tortuous, Don't confuse these words that sound so much
torturous alike and overlap in meaning but are nonetheless
different. *Tortuous* means crooked or devious, full
of twists and turns. *Torturous* means involving
torture, painful or distorted.

A woman goes to the governor and begs him to
pardon her husband, and the governor asks, "Why

is he in prison?"

"He stole a loaf of bread," she explains.
The governor asks, "Is he a good father?"
She responds, "He's rotten, he drinks, he
gambles, he hits the kids."
"Well, why do you want him back?" the
governor inquires.
She says, "We're out of bread again."

Tour de France TOOR d' FROHNS
Avoid: TOOR d' FRANS

If you want to anglicize the name of the French bicycle race, call it the Tour of France. Since no one would ever say TOOR dee FRANS, TOOR d' FRANS sounds like an uncomfortable hybrid. Names deserve to retain their native pronunciation to the extent practical and will thus help convey the authenticity and flavor of what they denote. The problem probably arises because speakers see the French words *Tour* and *France* and imagine them to be English. It's usually better to avoid hybrid pronunciations when you can. That's why I'll say "the hunchback of NOH-truh DAHM" but "the running back of NOH-tur DAYM", not NOH-truh DAYM.

tournament TUR-nuh-m'nt or TOOR-nuh-m'nt

transient TRAN-zee-int, TRAN-see-int or TRAN-shint

travail truh-VAIL or TRAV-ail
Don't say: truh-VY

traverse truh-VURS or TRAV-urs

triathlon trigh-ATH-lahn
Don't say: trigh-ATH-uh-lahn
See: **decathlon, pentathlon** and **biathlon**

Connecticut's Willie Pep twice held the World Featherweight title, and had one of the longest careers ever in prize-fighting, winning 230 of 242 fights. I visited their training camp before Willie took on Hogan Kid Bassey of Nigeria. Pep was near the end of his career and was ten years older than the one-time British Empire feather-weight champ. Willie lost that one.

triskaidekaphobia TRIS-kigh-DEK-uh-**PHOH**-bee-uh
Having been born on the 13th, I could never afford to be afraid of the number 13.

try and Avoid this construction. Try to avoid, that is. Don't try and avoid it.

Tuesday See: -day

turquoise TUR-koyz or TUR-kwoyz

Tuskegee tus-KEE-gee
(Alabama and Don't say: tus-kuh-GEE
University)

ubiquitous yoo-BIK-wih-tus
Don't say: oo-BIK-wih-tus

ukulele YOO-kuh-**LAY**-lee
This word is rarely mispronounced but often misspelled.

unique Unique means one of a kind, so avoid expressions like "very unique."

usury YOO-zhuh-ree
Don't say: YOO-zuh-ree or YOO-suh-ree

Always borrow from a pessimist. He doesn't expect to be repaid anyway.

No one is sure when Satchel Paige was born but it's estimated he was 59 when he took the mound for the last time, throwing three shutout innings for the Kansas City A's in 1965. "Age is a case of mind over matter. If you don't mind, it don't matter," he pointed out, showing why he was famous for his words as well as his arm. Joe DiMaggio called Paige "the best and fastest pitcher I've ever faced."

vagary VAY-guh-ree or vuh-GAIR-ee

vagrant VAY-gr'nt
At the scene of an automobile accident, a vagrant asked one of the victims, "Have the police been here yet?"
"No."
"Has the insurance guy been here yet?"
"No."
Then he asked, "Would you mind if I lie down beside you?"

valet VAL-it, va-LAY or VAL-ay
From my Poppings of the Day column in the April, 1936 issue of *The Motorcyclist*:
"**Which reminds me**, I'm getting fat. Quit eating out and am reaching at a boarding house where the meals are bigger and better. The waitresses were too tough at the restaurants. If I didn't leave a tip every meal one girl would send me a statement at the end of the month, itemizing the days I'd missed. Boy, she was mean. And she would bring me swordfish without sharpening it first, and all that. Couldn't get salt and pepper there, either, as she said it was bad for my health. Said last year over 200,000 people died in the United States and all were found to be habitual users of salt and pepper! Quick, Jeeves, my sidecar!"

vanilla vuh-NIL-uh
Don't say: va-NIL-uh
The dentist found that nine-year old Johnny had a cavity. "What kind of filling would you like, Johnny?" he asked. "I don't care. I'll take vanilla or chocolate," he replied.

vase vays or vayz
Avoid: vahz

vaudeville VAWD-vil
Avoid: VAW-duh-vil

vehement VEE-uh-m'nt
Don't say: VEE-huh-m'nt
The *h* is silent in both *vehement* and *vehicle*.

vehicle VEE-ih-k'l
Don't say: VEE-HIH-k'l
*What vehicle costs over $500 a mile?
A shopping cart!*

Venezuela VEN-uh-**ZWAY**-luh
Some say: VEN-zuh-**WAIL**-uh. They shouldn't.

verbal Don't confuse with *oral*. *Verbal* means in words, not necessarily spoken words. A "verbal agreement" could be written or oral; either way it's in words.

versatile VURS-uh-t'l
Avoid: VURS-uh-tyl
See: **docile, fertile, fragile, futile, hostile, juvenile, mobile, servile** and **volatile.** Textile, juvenile and **domicile,** however, have bucked the trend of these words pronounced with a short *i* and are often pronounced with a long *i* as in Britain.

vertebrae **VUR**-tuh-BREE
Don't say: **VUR**-tuh-BRAY
See: **alumnae, antennae** and **larvae**

veteran VET-ur-in or VEH-trun

veterinarian VET-ur-uh-**NAIR**-ee-uhn
Don't say: VEH-truh-**NAIR**-ee-uhn

The shortening of *veteran* from three syllables to two would seem to justify shortening *veterinarian* from six to five. The temptation to shorten a six-syllable word is hard to resist, but careful speakers avoid the shortcut.

A New London man had a pet rabbit. It got sick one day so he took it to the veterinarian and the vet proceeded to examine it. "I can't understand, Doc," the man said. "I give my rabbit the best of care. I even give it goat's milk to drink." The vet no sooner heard this than he handed the rabbit back to his owner.

"No wonder," he said, "you should know better than to use that greasy kid stuff on your hare."

via VY-uh or VEE-uh (VY sounds like *vie*, rhymes with *my*)

vice versa VY-suh VUR-suh (VY sounds like *vie*)
Avoid: VYS VUR-suh

The *vice* in *vice versa* is not the same *vice* as in *vice squad*, and vice versa.

vichyssoise VIH-she-**SWAHZ** or VEE-she-**SWAHZ**
Don't say: VIH-she-**SWAH**
See: **coup de grâce.**

victuals VIT-'lz
Don't say: VIK-tyoo-uls

vinaigrette   VIN-uh-**GRET**
Don't say: VIN-uh-g'r-**ET**

They say you can catch more flies with honey than with vinegar, but who needs flies?

viola   vee-OH-luh
Don't say: vy-OH-luh (vy sounds like *vie*, rhymes with *my*); unless you mean baseball lefthander, Frank Viola.

visa   VEE-zuh
Don't say: VEE-suh or VIGH-zuh

vis-à-vis   VEEZ-uh-VEE
Don't say: VIZ-uh-VEE or VEES-uh-VEE

Interviewing Jackie Robinson, one of the greatest baseball players ever. I asked him if retirement gave him any trouble with his weight. Jackie said, "I never step on the scale. I can tell my weight by my belt."

viscount   VY-kownt (VY sounds like *vie*)
Don't say: VIS-kownt or VIZ-kownt

volatile   VAHL-uh-t'l
Don't say: VAHL-uh-TYL (TYL sounds like *tile*) See: **docile, fertile, fragile, futile, hostile, juvenile, mobile, servile** and **versatile. Textile, juvenile** and **domicile,** however, have bucked the trend of these words pronounced with a short *i* and are often pronounced with a long *i* as in Britain.

voir dire   vwahr DEER
Don't say: vwahr DIGH-ur
Definition: examination of prospective jurors

voyeur   voy-UR
Don't say: vwah-UR or voy-OOR
See: **connoisseur, entrepreneur** and other words from the French ending in *eur*: **saboteur, auteur, raconteur, chauffeur, provocateur, restaurateur, hauteur, liqueur, de rigeur.**

wail, whale   The *h* in *wh* at the beginning of a word is usually aspirated (e.g. *whisper*) and is denoted in dictionaries by *hw*. With some *wh* words, such as *white* and *why*, the *hw* sound has come to sound not merely fastidious but affected, and the *h* is better unheard. In a few, it's the *w* that's silent (*who*, *whole* and *whore*). For those like *whisper*, it may just be too much fun, too much a part of their onomatopoeic effect, not to aspirate the *wh* (e.g. *whirl* and *whisk*). And one may not want to erase the distinction between *whalers* and *wailers* and between *whither* and *wither*.

Walesa, Lech   vuh-WEN-suh, LEK

wanton   WAHN-t'n
Avoid: WAHNT-'n

Don't rhyme with *wonton*. Our family used to go to a Chinese restaurant in Hartford because they chopped their own suey. When we asked for soup, the waiter asked what kind. "Wonton," I replied. He brought us two thousand pounds of soup.

warrantee   One who issues a guaranty for a product guarantees that product. So why can't one who issues a warranty be said to warrantee that product? Many in business certainly think so and make avid use of *warrantee* as a verb. The absence of such a verb from dictionaries has been no restraint. Nor has the availability of the verb *warrant*. Of course, language is constantly adding new words for far less reason. Just keep in mind that *warrantee* comes with no *pedigree,* let alone *warranty.* It's not even a very helpful word, more spin than substance as used. How much does it really tell you to be told that a business provides a warranty for a product? It's what's in the warranty that matters.

Wednesday See: -**day**

Wesleyan WES-lee-in
Don't say: WEZ-lee-in

Westminster wes-MIN-st'r (for London's famous Abbey)
Don't say: west-MIN-st'r or west-**MIN**-ih-ST'R

whither, wither See: **wail**

wiliness WY-lee-nis (WY sounds like why)
Don't say: WIL-ee-nis

Author James Gwaitney's new novel was not selling in Philadelphia so he inserted the following classified ad in the two metropolitan newspapers: "YOUNG MILLIONAIRE, good-looking, wishes to meet with view to matrimony, a girl like the heroine in Enduring Young Charms, written by James Gwaitney." Within 24 hours the book was sold out.

Woburn
(Massachusetts) WOO-burn
Don't say: WOH-burn

Wodehouse, P.G. WOOD-hous
Appearance to the contrary, not: WOHD-hous

Wolcott
(Connecticut) WOOL-k't
Don't say: WAL-kaht

wreak reek

Don't say: rek
Definition: to inflict (e.g. to wreak havoc on an enemy).

I was arrested for making 21 straight wrong predictions. So many lost money on wagers that it was the scandal of the day. Seriously, Ted Williams and I both agreed to police blotters of ourselves on a visit to the state prison in Wethersfield for a sports banquet.

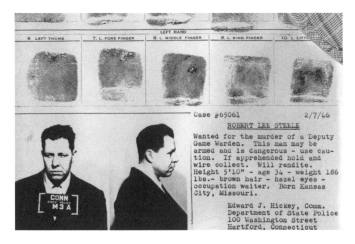

Case #65061   2/7/46

ROBERT LEE STEELE

Wanted for the murder of a Deputy Game Warden. This man may be armed and is dangerous - use caution. If apprehended hold and wire collect. Will rendite. Height 5'10" - age 34 - weight 186 lbs.- brown hair - hazel eyes - occupation waiter. Born Kansas City, Missouri.

Edward J. Hickey, Comm.
Department of State Police
100 Washington Street
Hartford, Connecticut

Xavier ZAY-vee-ur, ZAV-ee-ur or ZAYV-yur

Don't, generally, say: eks-AY-vee-ur or egg-ZAY-vee-ur. But some, like musician Xavier Cugat, pronounce it eks-AY-vee-ur. To the consternation of some, such as the editor of the Stafford Press, who, in the course of a 1944 piece on my eggs à la Steele recipe, wrote:

"Bob Steele of WTIC who annoys us by pronouncing Cugat's name improperly as Exayvier instead of properly Zayvier. However we'll forgive him that lapse for the pleasant dish he exposed us to." Hey, man, blame Cugat, not me!

xylophone ZY-luh-fohn (ZY rhymes with *my*)

Don't be baffled by the *x*. Consider it a *z*. That's the way it sounds in nearly all words starting with *x*. The only exceptions we've ever heard of are foreign names like *Xingu* (shing-GOO), a river in Brazil, *Xiu* (shoh), a Chinese name) and the unique word *Xmas*, which can be pronounced the same as *Christmas* or EKS-muhs. X-words that are hyphenated, of course, get the EKS sound, like *x-ray*.

yo Would you believe the Lone Ranger never said, "Hi-Ho, Silver, Away"? At least 99 out of a hundred people who remember "The Lone Ranger" from radio or TV will tell you the masked man signed off every show with that command, or "Hi-Oh.". But he didn't. What he said was "Hi-Yo, Silver, Away!" According to historian Irving Settel, the phrase "Hi-Yo Silver" was used as a password by American troops entering Algiers during World War II. "Hi-Ho" may have worked as well in that foreign context, but there's a lot of difference between a *yo* and a *ho*. Robert Louis Stevenson wrote, "Fifteen men on a dead man's chest/Yo ho ho and a bottle of rum," not "Ho ho ho." And Santa Claus isn't known for "Yo, yo, yo!" In the Disney classic, the Seven Dwarfs sang, "Heigh-Ho, Heigh-Ho/It's home from work we go."

Interviewing Jack Nicklaus at the Insurance City Open at Wethersfield Country Club. In all my years of covering sports I could never understand golf. My favorite shot is Scotch with very little soda and my favorite course is dessert. I never had a bird but I did hit a duck in flight once.

Ypsilanti   IP-sil-**AN**-tee
(Michigan)   Don't say: YIP-sil-**AN**-tee
When it starts a name, some treat Y more like a
consonant than a vowel. See: **Yvonne, Yvette, Yves**

Yvonne, Yvette   ee-VAHN, ee-VET
Don't say yuh-VAHN or yuh-VET
Same principle applies to *Yves* (eve)

zebra   One fellow who heard our explanation about the *z* sound in *x* words told us he never has any trouble pronouncing them correctly now. But he's having trouble spelling words like XEBRA.

XEBRA RLS

zero, O   If you have a zero in your phone number, or on most any other occasion, we think it's perfectly okay to pronounce it the same as the letter *O*, rather than "zero."

Ziegfeld   ZIG-feld

Don't say: ZIG-field

Forenz Ziegfeld (1867-1932), the American theatrical producer, was known for the Ziegfeld Follies.

zoology zoh-AHL-uh-jee

Don't say: zoo-AHL-uh-jee
The z is followed by double *o*, not by three of
them. There's no *zoo* in zoology.

A man who owned two seals liked to drive around
with them in his convertible. One day a police
officer stopped him and told him to take the seals
to the zoo. The next day the officer saw the man
and his seals again, stopped him again and said to
him, "I thought I told you to take those seals to
the zoo." The man replied, "I did just as you said.
Today I'm taking them to the beach."

The great New York
Giants running back
Frank Gifford led his
team to three NFL
title games and the
championship in
1956. Gifford was a
standout on defense
as well as offense.
Like yours truly, Frank
built a broadcasting
career on his
experience in
sports.

AFTERWORD

Lots of people will tell you they've been listening to Bob Steele all their lives. I truly have been listening to Bob Steele all of my life. And he has been listening to me. He does not always correct my mispronunciations. Sometimes he just looks me in the eye as if to say I'll give you three seconds to reconsider that pronunciation. It's especially disconcerting to be corrected when I've just used a word that I was rather proud of having used at all. I have vivid recollections of some of those times. For instance, I was initially pleased once to have used *eschewed* in precisely the right context. My father's brow knit itself together before I could make es SHOO past tense.

There are positive sides to being listened to by a word hawk. It's good for one's humility. And it certainly didn't make the family word-shy. My older brother Robert was originally an English major at Amherst College and later got to talk a lot in the U. S. House of Representatives. Younger brother Phil, co-author of this book, was an English teacher before he became a lawyer. I teach English. And youngest brother Steve has an uncanny ability to mimic the speech mannerisms of presidents and movie stars. Somebody taught him to attend to words.

Attention to words can be a contagious thing. It's a healthful contagion. I hope this book will gain the audience it deserves. For me it was compulsive reading. Not compulsory, but compulsive. I heard a voice from within saying, Don't speak another word until you have finished reading this book.

Paul Steele